What *Not* to Say

What *Not* to Say

Avoiding the Common Mistakes
That Can Sink Your Sermon

John C. Holbert and Alyce M. McKenzie

WESTMINSTER
JOHN KNOX PRESS
LOUISVILLE · KENTUCKY

© 2011 John C. Holbert and Alyce M. McKenzie

First edition
Published by Westminster John Knox Press
Louisville, Kentucky

11 12 13 14 15 16 17 18 19 20—10 9 8 7 6 5 4 3 2 1

Scripture quotations from the New Revised Standard Version of the Bible are copyright © 1989 by the Division of Christian Education of the National Council of the Churches of Christ in the U.S.A. and are used by permission.

Book design by Sharon Adams
Cover design by Eric Walljasper, Minneapolis, MN

Library of Congress Cataloging-in-Publication Data
Holbert, John C.
    What not to say : avoiding the common mistakes that can sink your sermon / John C. Holbert, Alyce M. McKenzie. — 1st ed.
        p. cm.
    Includes bibliographical references (p.   ).
    ISBN 978-0-664-23510-9 (alk. paper)
    1. Preaching. I. McKenzie, Alyce M., 1955– II. Title.
    BV4211.3.H655 2011
    251—dc23

                                                                    2011033184

♾ The paper used in this publication meets the minimum requirements of the American National Standard for Information Sciences—Permanence of Paper for Printed Library Materials, ANSI Z39.48-1992

Most Westminster John Knox Press books are available at special quantity discounts when purchased in bulk by corporations, organizations, and special-interest groups. For more information, please e-mail SpecialSales@wjkbooks.com.

Contents

128491

Introduction

A couple years ago, on a spring day in Dallas, we sat in a booth at Chili's restaurant on Knox Avenue having fish tacos. Our purpose was to discuss collaborating on a textbook on preaching.

"Do you think it's all been said before?" Alyce asked.

"Maybe, but not by us," John replied.

"But what could we offer that's new?" was the question in both our minds. After all, there are any number of very fine introductory texts that attempt to initiate new and nearly new preachers into the wonders and mysteries of this ancient act. Each of us is very familiar with these: books by Broadus, Lowry, Buttrick, Craddock, Long, Allen, and Wilson, to name the most-used of these introductions. These books have covered the many topics of preaching with clarity, care, and completeness. What could we possibly add to their efforts?

What we thought our book might offer may be summarized in four ways.

1. Diversity of gender perspectives. One of us is a man, and the other is a woman. There has been an ongoing discussion, at times a rather heated debate, among those who teach preaching, concerning the distinctions between a female presentation of the act of preaching and a male presentation, even beyond the older discussions surrounding gender differences in teaching anything. This book combines thoughts and insights from both sides of this gender divide. This is a first in an introductory text. We leave it to the reader to discern where differences may lie between us in the ways we go at this task. Our hope is that you will find value in the distinctions you discern.

2. Practical experience based on years of teaching. We wanted to get down to the very core of an effective sermon and focus our attention squarely there. Just what makes a sermon "good"? When we asked this question of one another, it became apparent that it was far easier to remember what made sermons we had preached and heard *not* so good! In the course of the brainstorming session, one of us mentioned the TLC show *What Not to Wear*. We began to entertain the idea of an introductory book on sermon preparation called *What Not to Say*. We found that what not to say was so much easier to describe than what one ought to say. Our goal is to give very direct advice out of the store of our combined sixty years of preaching and over forty years of teaching others how to preach.

3. Brevity and accessibility. We wanted brevity in our presentation, because we had many audiences in mind. Both of us are ordained United Methodist elders and thus are often asked to teach in regional Course of Study schools where persons not readily able to spend three or four full-time years preparing for ministry get only a two-week course to get them ready to preach in their churches. We wanted a book that we could use and that would prove brief, accurate, practical, and usable again and again. Also, we regularly are asked to do refresher workshops for clergy who have been at the task for some time but have grown stale, having fallen into one or more of the many ruts that the Sunday round too often presents. "Use this," we wanted to say, as a primer and reminder for the task you have been called to perform. And, of course, for our own students at the seminary, we wanted a short and readily accessible book that could remind them after their graduation about some of the things we tried to teach them while they were here.

4. Something fun to read. Perhaps most important of all, we wanted a fun book, one that presented its material in a lighthearted style that could make a reader laugh at the same time that she was learning a thing or two. We know all too well how dangerous it is to set out to write something that tries to be funny. It runs the dual risk of silliness, hence triviality, and finally not being funny after all. We accept that risk, because our own experience as teachers is that without humor the possibility of learning and the joy of teaching are lost and squandered, or at least blunted. We both hope you will find this primer, if not a barrel of guffaws, at least worthy of a chortle or two.

We have divided our work into eight chapters. Alyce wrote the chapters on God, people, endings, and illustrative stories and images. John wrote the chapters on beginnings, middles, the Bible, and the self. We chose those things that especially interested us and that we thought we had special insights into, though each of us could have switched the assignments and still been happy. We are well aware that we might have cut the homiletical pie in other ways, broaching other subjects that have been addressed in those introductions already mentioned. However, we are convinced that these eight subjects lie at the very heart of any sermon and that careful attention to them will lead a preacher to the central issues of the preaching task.

Note that we have created a video, located at http://HolbertMcKenzie.wjkbooks.com, that illustrates many of the suggestions we have made in the text. It is free for all and easy to use. When you read, for example, some suggestions for what not to say about the beginnings of a sermon, you need watch only the section of the video on beginnings to listen to examples of ways we think sermons ought, or ought not, to begin. The illustrations are hardly exhaustive, but we do think they are representative and can serve you as you think about the several parts of a sermon of your own.

We are grateful for the colleagues who assisted us as speakers on this video: Rev. Herbert S. Coleman II, director of recruitment and admissions, Perkins School of Theology; Dr. Hugo Magallanes, Associate Professor of Christianity and Cultures, Perkins School of Theology; Shellie Ross, student intern at Wesley-Rankin Community Center, Dallas; and Cassandra Wilson, student intern at Glide Memorial United Methodist Church, San Francisco. The two of us appear in the video as well: Dr. John C. Holbert, Lois Craddock Perkins Professor of Homiletics, Perkins School of Theology; and Dr. Alyce M. McKenzie, George W. and Nell Ayers LeVan Professor of Preaching and Worship, Perkins School of Theology.

So here is the book we dreamed up at Chili's during that long-ago lunch. We would like to dedicate it to the faculty, staff, and students of Perkins School of Theology. That first group of remarkable scholars and teachers make coming to work a pleasure. The second group provides the glue that holds the place together. The third gives us our work, listens to our attempts to share what we know, and are the final judges of whether what we have tried to do has, in fact, gotten done. To all these colleagues and friends, past and present, we offer our most profound thanks.

Chapter 1

What Not to Say (and What to Say) about God

Your God is too small.

J. B. Phillips

$\mathcal{S}$ometimes I feel annoyed at God as I face the task of preaching. Sometimes I feel like God has left me in an awkward position, because if I had more facts I could do a better job defending God to certain people in certain situations. If I had more facts, I could square my shoulders, look sufferers and doubters in the eye, and proclaim, "I know everything there is to know about God. I am more worthy than Moses, who had to hide in the cleft of a rock and see God's backside. I am purer than Isaiah in the temple who cried out, 'Woe is me! . . . For I am a man of unclean lips, and I live among a people of unclean lips!' (Isa. 6:5). I am more discerning and righteous than the apostle Paul, who said we all see in a glass but darkly. Not me. I can look at God face-to-face, right here, right now. I know everything there is to know about God. I know why the innocent suffer. I know exactly how prayer works and why some people experience a physical cure and others a spiritual healing. I know exactly whom you will meet after death and what the schedule of daily activities in the afterlife will be. I know what will be on the menu at the messianic banquet. I know the mind of God."

Some people we encounter expect a pastor to be able to say all the above with a straight face. Some people assume that a pastor is the answer man or the answer woman. While that may be who some want us to be, it's not who I believe we are called to be. As human beings we don't have all the answers, and we dread those questions about God we don't have the answer for: "How could God be good and allow suffering?" "Why did my friend's cancer get worse when the whole church was praying?" When such questions come our way, it's crucial that we not then say to ourselves, "If people have these questions, I'd better answer them all in my sermons."

1

If nobody were listening, it wouldn't matter so much what we preachers said or didn't say about God. But believe it or not, people actually listen to what we preachers say. They listen to the way we portray God, and they think about how that applies to their daily lives, both their good days and their days of misfortune.

In response to sermons, they may think things like the following:

- I'm tired of getting beat up, but I guess God wants me to take up my cross and hang in there.
- I guess the reason I'm struggling financially is because I need more faith.
- I did so well with my investments this week. God is really blessing me and my family.
- My wife and I must have done something to deserve the miscarriage of our child, but what?
- It hurts to lose my child, but the preacher says everything that happens is part of God's plan.
- If I can learn to pray expecting great things, my diabetes will improve, my wife will come back to me, and I'll be able to find a job.
- The preacher says that God didn't cause my accident, but that God allowed it to happen. Either way, I'm angry.

Since people are listening to the ways we depict God in our sermons and applying what we say to the specific situations of their daily lives, we need to be very careful, both about our unintentional messages and about our intentional messages. Unintentional theological messages can be a problem. They happen when we imply statements we don't mean to about God. For example, I didn't mean to convey that God automatically responds to our prayers by improving our circumstances. But I used an illustration about a man sitting in McDonald's, depressed and jobless, who happened to pick up the paper someone had left, read about a job in the classified section, and apply for and get the job that day. Suppose that a lot of my examples, from week to week, are happy-ending examples. What does that convey about God and how God relates to us? Unintentional theological statements are one problem. They often come through our choices of illustrations.

I wish people would be bolder sometimes. I wish they would follow us across the parking lot to ask a question: "Preacher, did you really mean to say that? Because I heard you say that salvation is the reward for good works. I heard that the motivation for individual kindness and acts of justice is because it makes us feel better. I heard that faith is a personal matter, between me and God. I heard that good health is a sign of God's blessing. I heard the flipside—that my poor health is a sign of God's curse. I heard that if I increase my pledge this year God will arrange the circumstances of my life so that I can pay it."

While it may be true that people hear what they want to hear, it's also true that sometimes they hear things because we say them.

Even worse than giving unintentional messages about God are those instances when the preacher intentionally depicts God in ways that are not faithful to the whole canon of the biblical witness and in ways that are damaging to the faith of her hearers. In the syllabus for my introduction to preaching class, I include a list of statements about God under the heading "Theological Pitfalls: Please Don't Preach This!" The list consists of several messages about God that preachers either intentionally or unwittingly preach that, in my view, are not faithful to the canonical sweep of the biblical witness and that do pastoral damage.

- If you had more faith, you would be healed and your problems would disappear.
- Faith automatically brings happy endings, healings, job opportunities, restored relationships, and so forth.
- Living faithfully is a very simple matter.
- God has everything all worked out; if we would just cooperate, life would be fine.
- Misfortunes come directly from God as punishments or teaching moments.
- There are no accidents.
- All suffering is a cross we must bear to be faithful disciples.
- Faith is a purely personal matter. Talking about issues of public life in the pulpit is mixing faith and politics.
- When good things happen, God is smiling on us.
- God helps those who help themselves.

After reading this list, one student, an inveterate jokester, raised his hand and said, "Thanks, Dr. M. Now I have the themes for my sermon series for Lent! Now could you give me a text for each one?" The answer to such a question is "Yes, I could." I could find at least one Scripture verse to support each of the above statements, either directly or indirectly. That is no reason to preach any of them, however. As the saying goes, "A text without a context is a pretext." As Martin Luther is said to have remarked, "Even the devil can quote Scripture."

But it takes so much time to know the whole Bible and exegete one's congregational context. Proof-texting, choosing one verse and ignoring both the immediate and larger biblical contexts, could be such a timesaver for the busy pastor in preparing her sermons. It also increases the chances that she would say all sorts of things about God that are not faithful to the canon and that are not good news, with its inextricable blend of challenge and comfort.

I think it was theologian Gerhard Ebeling who once said, "Theology exists to make preaching as difficult as it needs to be." At a recent faculty dinner, I quoted that to a colleague who teaches theology. He was taking a forkful of Italian cream cake at the time, and he stopped it midway from plate to mouth to protest, "That's not the only reason theology exists!" Point taken. But I am a professor of preaching, and my role is to be a theological gadfly. My job is to nudge students to think about what they are saying about God and our response to God. My job is to ask in sermon feedback sessions and to write in the margins of their sermons, "Did you really mean to say that about God? And about our response to God?" In return, students are free to download my picture from the faculty Web site, print it out, and place it in the center of a dartboard. I'll understand. But I'm not going to stop asking them when they've finished preaching, "Did you really mean to say that about God?" And I'm not going to stop asking myself the same question as I prepare my own sermons.

It's hard to take words back once we've said them. I have a pastor friend who does a lot of guest preaching. He always takes a tube of toothpaste and a toothbrush with him in case the congregation calls on him to preach a children's sermon. He calls the children up and tells them he forgot to brush his teeth that morning. He squeezes the toothpaste out onto the toothbrush, then decides maybe it's not good manners to brush his teeth in front of the whole congregation. He then tries to get the children to help him squeeze the toothpaste back into the tube. It's kind of a messy sermon, but it gets the point across. Once words leave our lips, it's impossible to retract them.

The apostle Paul advised us to be imitators of him, but I actually think many of us preachers instead choose to imitate the apostle Peter on the Mount of Transfiguration. At the first sign of a blinding light, something we don't understand, we begin babbling and building bad theological booths, flimsy ones that can't bear the brunt of life's foul weather.

What Not to Say about God

There are three things I most certainly do not want to say about God to my listeners, either intentionally or unintentionally. The first is that God is directly responsible for everything that happens to us. The second and third flow from the first: that God is the source of all our good abundance and that God is the source of all our suffering.

These are three weeds I am convinced we need to dig up and remove from our preachers' garden. Each has theological roots, theological assumptions that lie beneath its surface. Each has pastoral shoots, effects, often damaging, that stem from those roots.

God Is the Direct Cause of All That Happens to You

Theological Roots

The Scriptures we call the Old and New Testaments affirm God as the creator, sustainer, and redeemer of our world and humankind. God hovers over the chaos and speaks the world into existence in Genesis. The heavens proclaim the glory of God in Psalms. God chooses a covenant people. God delivers them from Pharaoh. God provides prophets and sages. God desires that Israel be a light to all the nations. God becomes incarnate in Jesus Christ, teaching, healing, living, dying, rising, and living again. God's Spirit guides the newly forming church in Acts. In the book of Revelation, God holds up a vision of the end of the age, of justice and vindication, when all tears will be wiped away.

The God we meet in Scripture is both transcendent and involved. The God of the Old Testament manifests power and glory through the vast scope of nature. At the same time, God shows a concern for and relation to history and to a particular people within it. In the New Testament we meet this same God, Alpha and Omega, now manifest in the "Son," Jesus of Nazareth, through whom God's insistence on justice and mercy for human beings is shown, through whom God's power to save even from death is revealed, and in whom God's sovereignty over all creation will one day be fully and visibly established. God can be affirmed as a sovereign God in the sense that God's plan to redeem and restore the world and humankind will not ultimately be thwarted.

Christian theological reflection on Scripture affirms that our sovereign God, as the creator and ruler of all, transcends all creaturely limits and characteristics. God is transcendent, the source of all creation, not a creature. God is not dependent on or merely an effect of other things. At the same time, Christian theology has affirmed that this transcendent God is deeply related to and active within the natural world and the course of history.

In classical theological constructions, the doctrine of creation has to do with understanding God as the author or source of the world. The doctrine of providence has to do with understanding God as working in and with the world (Wood 2008, 76). Traditional doctrines of providence, especially in Western theological traditions, have emphasized God's control over all events, assuming God is the source of all events that happen to us. They have portrayed a universal order in which everything that happens is specifically arranged by God to serve God's good purposes (Wood 2008, 15).

Many people use this unquestioned assumption that everything that happens to them is God's will to help them interpret the events of their daily lives. Those of us in denominations influenced by the Protestant Reformers have a long history of being influenced by this understanding of God's relationship to the world.

An insistence that God is in control of all events fueled John Calvin's notion of double predestination. Drawing on Augustine's understanding of total depravity and divine election, he reasoned that human beings are unable to either will or do good because of the fall. He then asked how are we to account for the fact that some respond to God's unmerited Grace and are saved while others do not respond and are not saved. His answer was that if some people do not turn to God and live righteous lives, it is because God did not intend for them to do so. If others do, it is because God intended for them to do so. So everything that does and doesn't happen is ascribed to God's will. Luther, while he believed we are totally depraved, believed that God through Christ agrees to view us as righteous (imputes righteousness to us). He left open the question of why it is that not all people accept their acceptance by God. Wesley rejected predestination in favor of the belief that while we can resist God's Grace and reject our salvation, salvation is offered to all.

Ascribing to God everything that happens to us enables us to feel some sense of control in an unpredictable world. But it is an illusory sense of control. In seeking to safeguard God's control over all events, it does damage to God's goodness. This approach also factors out the role of freewill in both the good and the evil that happen in the world. Despite these deficiencies, "It must have been God's will" remains our default position, the knee-jerk refrain that springs to our lips as the mallot of misfortune strikes our lives.

Pastoral Shoots: Damage to Listeners' Lives

Many of the pastorally damaging messages we send from the pulpit are the result of our attempts to ascribe everything that happens, in the wider world and in our own little world, to the direct will and action of God.

On this basis, many pastors tell people that the deaths of young people, tragic accidents, and natural disasters are all part of our lives because they are the will of God: "She was so young and had so much of life in front of her, but I guess God wanted another flower in the heavenly bouquet." (Or maybe somebody drank his breakfast, crossed the median, and hit her head on.)

This kind of theological self-medication is what people are already administering to themselves. We need to confiscate it, not confirm it. We've all heard people comfort themselves with statements like "God intended this tragedy to happen for the greater good." We recognize it because we've all probably tried to clasp that cold comfort ourselves at one time or another. Diane, a pastor in a suburban Dallas church, visited an elderly woman in a rehab center whose failing eyesight had caused her to fall and break her hip. An attendant came into the room during Diane's visit and said cheerily, "Oh, God intended that this happen to Jean so that she would come here and be such an uplifting influence on the other patients." If I were Jean, I'd be thinking, "Thanks a lot, God."

By this logic, God intends some people to die in violent traffic accidents so that other people can have their transplanted eyes and hearts. God intended one of my students' younger brothers to poke him in the eye with a pencil when they were barely out of the toddler stage so that my student would know the spiritual growth that comes from living his whole life with one eye rather than two. And these are just personal examples. What about the actions of violent leaders or the effects of systemic evil like racism or homophobia? What about the effects of earthquakes and tsunamis and hurricanes?

I was leading a workshop recently titled "Living by Biblical Wisdom in a Self-Help Society." We were comparing the rather optimistic wisdom of Proverbs, which says if you live wisely, your life will be secure, with the darker wisdom of Job, which features a main character whose life contradicts that optimistic view.

We had been talking about how the book of Job never answers the question we most want answered: Why do the innocent suffer? We talked about how, in our minds, there must be some explanation for human suffering. It has to be my fault, your fault, or God's fault. I told the story of a young man whose wife miscarried. He kept repeating the same question ("What did we do to deserve this?") followed by a statement: "We must have done something to deserve this."

At the break a woman came up to me. She didn't say, "Hello, I'm Marla. How are you?" or "I'm really enjoying the workshop so far." She simply looked at me and said, "Human beings would rather feel guilty than out of control." It was a great conversation starter. It led us to a place of agreement about what scares us the most: that sometimes things happen randomly and unpredictably despite our best efforts at creating a safe, secure, sanitized life for ourselves. That's what Job's friends feared above all. Because if tragedy could happen to him, it could happen to them. They figured there must be some invisible but potent difference between him and them. At the end of the book, the God of the whirlwind points out to Job—using images of creatures he has never even imagined that swim beneath the sea and tromp across the land—that the world is a much more complex place than Job could ever imagine. God rubs Job's nose in the reality that divine retribution is a human invention. He assures Job that they (God and Job) can live with danger and randomness because they will face it and live it together.

The pastoral damage that occurs when we ascribe all events to God is described this way by theologian Charles Wood: "It encourages passivity and resignation in those who are relatively powerless and intensifies their sense of guilt and worthlessness, while at the same time fostering a sense of well-being and self-satisfaction among the relatively powerful" (Wood 2008, 76).

To be told that all that happens to you is the will of God can make comfortable people passive, and complacent and poor people passive and self-loathing. Some congregations are filled with people whose lives are generally safe and materially comfortable, interrupted occasionally by an unexpected medical diagnosis or the death of a loved one. They have time in-between mishaps to regroup. They have an economic cushion to soften the sting of the slings and arrows.

What if you are preaching to a group of people whose lives are not generally safe and materially comfortable? What if pretty much everything about their lives seems beyond their control? What if they habitually feel out of control, at others' mercy, helpless, and in danger? To be told that everything that happens to me is God's will leads to one of two responses, possibly both: a habitual, perpetual self-loathing of great intensity ("I must be awful to deserve such an awful life") or an even more intense loathing for God ("God must be awful to dole out such a miserable life to me").

The insistence that God is the direct cause of all that happens in our lives leads to two other claims: God is the source of abundance in our lives, defined in largely material terms, and God is the source of suffering in our lives.

God Is the Source of Your Abundance

Theological Roots

The promise that positive thoughts yield positive outcomes has been around for centuries. It's no secret, despite Rhonda Byrne's recent book titled *The Secret*. It's a half-truth. Things do go better when we think positive thoughts. But when preachers bring God into it, they enter the land of half-truths. They begin to promise people something that neither the full biblical witness nor life supports: that God guarantees abundance for them, defined as physical health, financial prosperity, fulfilling relationships, rewarding pursuits, and a long and happy life. Preachers can then imply (and sometimes state outright) that if their listeners do not possess these things, it's their fault, not God's. Preachers are then tempted to wag their finger at their people, scolding them for assumed internal shortcomings on the basis of their external circumstances: "If you only had more faith, you would be physically healed, your relationships would be happy, and you would be financially prosperous."

To say that God wants abundance for us is true. God is the source of our abundance if we are talking about the spiritual abundance of joy, peace, and forgiveness that are the unmerited gifts of our gracious God. What I don't want to say about God is the claim by prosperity Gospel preachers: that when we receive material prosperity, it is God's blessing for our right thinking and believing.

Yet there are biblical texts that, on first glance, seem to support this notion. The book of Deuteronomy, portions of which may date from the eighth century BCE, depicts Moses telling the Israelites that if they obey God, they will enter and claim the promised land (Deut. 6:16–19), but that if they do not, their disobedience will result in misfortune. Many of the prophets interpret misfortune and invasion by foreign powers as the result of that disobedience, but they promise restoration of land and covenant favor if the people turn back to God.

The book of Proverbs, collated in the postexilic period, promises the young that if they seek wisdom and work hard, they will find a degree of prosperity and a good reputation and be able to contribute to the stability of the community. Jesus promises in the Gospel of John, "I have come that they may have life and have it abundantly" (John 10:10).

In all these cases there is a cause-effect relationship between righteousness and positive outcomes that are material as well as spiritual. But a degree of moral effort and obedience are required. In all these cases, the good of the community is one of the benefits. All these cases call for a denial of our short-term gratification in order for God's purposes to be worked out.

This is different from the message that if we think right thoughts, pray right prayers, and realize that the universe yearns to give us our heart's desire, we will receive it. Magical thinking, whose goal is self-gratification, undergirds much New Age self-help literature and prosperity gospel preaching. The primary difference between the Bible's wisdom and this secular wisdom is that biblical wisdom is directed toward the shalom of the community, and it regards wisdom as a gift from God that has God as its destination.

Pastoral Shoots: Potential Damage to Listeners' Lives

The damage that prosperity gospel preaching can do is to cause people to doubt God's goodness when things don't go well for them despite their best efforts and thoughts. It can cause comfortable people to be complacent about the sufferings of others. Many prosperity preachers preach their message to people who seem materially comfortable and middle class. They tell them that if they think positive thoughts, that if they believe in God's power to bring them their best life now, their finances, relationships, and futures will prosper. This is more likely to be a self-fulfilling prophecy if I already have the material means to pursue my dreams. If I have the settled middle-class lifestyle that is conducive to being able to control my own time and limit my obligations to others, conditions are optimal for my accomplishing a set of self-directed goals. Telling people that if they send you money God will bless their lives and your ministry doesn't seem quite as heinous if the people to whom you're preaching won't much feel the loss. But what about when a prosperity preacher with an expensive wardrobe, a selection of luxury cars, and several homes holds up his lifestyle as proof of the validity of his message? What about when poor people send rich preachers money because of what rich preachers say about God, about how God operates, and about who God is and will be for them?

God Is the Source of Suffering in Our Lives

Theological Roots

The biblical understanding of the source of suffering in human life is a canonical tapestry with four primary threads. One is that we bring suffering on ourselves by our disobedience to God. We make idolatrous choices that put our human will in place of God's and thereby repeatedly bring suffering and sin into our world. So Adam and Eve are evicted from the garden, and the pattern of poor choices continues with the murder of Cain, the tower of Babel, and the careers of various patriarchs and matriarchs, all marred by periodic faithlessness, poor parenting, thinking, and acting guided by parts of the body other than the brain, and general shady dealings. God, meanwhile, is at work throughout the Old Testament doing damage control, offering a covenant relationship and guidelines for community living that minimize conflict and misery, and offering forgiveness and a new start when the covenant is repeatedly broken by human sin. God sends the prophets to warn the kings and wealthy oppressors of the poor. We are reminded, over and over again in the book of Proverbs, that folly leads to poverty and death: "Those who despise the word bring destruction on themselves, but those who respect the commandment will be rewarded" (Prov. 13:13). God sends Woman Wisdom to warn the fools. The warning is always the same: You will bring suffering on yourself and your community if you are disobedient to God.

The book of Ecclesiastes depicts an inscrutable God responsible for enjoyment and injustice alike, who is to be revered and not challenged: "For God is in heaven and you upon earth; therefore let your words be few" (Eccl. 5:2).

Jesus' teachings focus on repentance as a response to God's offering of the kingdom through his ministry and teaching. Disciples are those who not only believe but who do the will of God. They change their behavior. Discipleship, while it ultimately brings joy, can lead to suffering. A life of service involves sacrifice, inconvenience, risk, opposition, and even death.

This first thread doesn't ascribe suffering to God's direct agency. Rather, it emphasizes that we bring misery to ourselves and others by our actions. Three other strands of the tapestry of biblical views of human suffering attribute it to God. I don't buy any of them as is. I wouldn't preach any of them as is. I think all three of them confuse the effects God can bring about from suffering with God's actually causing that suffering.

- Punishment: God sends suffering to punish us for our disobedience.
- Pop Quiz: God sends suffering to discipline, strengthen, and teach us.
- Power Demo: God allows suffering so God's power may be made manifest in our weakness.

Punishment: God sends suffering to punish us for our disobedience.   Immediately after the prohibition of idolatry in Deuteronomy 5:9, God declares, "For I the Lord your God am a jealous God, punishing children for the iniquity of parents, to the third and fourth generation of those who reject me, but showing steadfast love to the thousandth generation of those who love me and keep my commandments." Hebrews 12:5 tells the believer, "My child, do not regard lightly the discipline of the Lord, or lose heart when you are punished by him." Nathan informs David that the child that results from his adultery with Bathsheba will die because of his sins (2 Sam. 12:14). The prophets exhort the Israelites that the repeated invasions of foreign powers are the result of the nation's mistreatment of the poor and hypocrisy before God. A strong strain of thought running through Deuteronomy and Proverbs that if you obey God you will prosper has a flip side: that if you do not obey, you will not prosper. Job's friends insist that he would not be suffering if he had not committed some heinous sin (Job 22:3–5). We see in the Gospels the notion that if you are disabled, ill, or poor, your condition is the result of your sins. "Who sinned, this man or his parents, that he was born blind?" (John 9:2). When Jesus says, "I have come to call not the righteous but sinners" (Mark 2:17) he is talking about those who are on the bottom economic and social rung—the poor, the disabled, the outcast—whom those higher up take theological comfort in labeling as sinners. They must be sinners, because all these sufferings are, after all, God's punishment for sin.

Pop Quiz: God sends suffering to discipline, strengthen, and teach us.   When I was a child and things weren't going well, my grandmother would say, "These things are given us to test us." Given by whom? I would wonder. Scripture tells us that they are given by God. God tests the Israelites in the wilderness to humble them and to see what is in their hearts, whether they will keep his commandments (Deut. 8:2). Deuteronomy 13:3 tells us that when we are tempted to idolatry, it is God testing us to know whether we indeed love the Lord our God with all our heart and soul. Similar motivations and actions by God are recorded in Judges 3:4, Hebrews 12:7–11, and James 1:3.

The author of Psalm 51, a psalm traditionally ascribed to a repentant King David, sings,

> Purge me with hyssop, and I shall be clean;
>   wash me, and I shall be whiter than snow.
> Let me hear joy and gladness;
>   let the bones that you have crushed rejoice.
> Hide your face from my sins,
>   and blot out all my iniquities.
>
> (vv. 7–9)

In the same vein, the author of Hebrews writes, "My child, do not regard lightly the discipline of the Lord, or lose heart when you are punished by him; for the Lord disciplines those whom he loves, and chastises every child whom he accepts" (Heb. 12:5–6).

God tests our faith by sending suffering, and, if we respond with faith, God deepens our character and our faith. Romans 5 teaches us that "suffering produces endurance, and endurance produces character, and character produces hope, and hope does not disappoint us because God's love has been poured into our hearts through the Holy Spirit that has been given to us" (Rom. 5:3–5).

By this understanding of God, a preacher is authorized to say, "This is your cross, sister. All suffering is a cross God sends you to strengthen you for God's service." This makes it sound like pain and wounds and misery are good in and of themselves—that when I'm suffering, God is happy.

Power Demo: God allows suffering so God's power may be made manifest in our weakness.   In John 9:2–3, Jesus is walking along and passes a man blind from birth. His disciples ask him, "Rabbi, who sinned, this man or his parents, that he was born blind?" Jesus replies, "Neither this man nor his parents sinned; he was born blind so that God's works might be revealed in him."

The apostle Paul found comfort in this understanding in dealing with his struggles and his mysterious "thorn in the flesh":

> Therefore, to keep me from being too elated, a thorn was given me in the flesh, a messenger of Satan to torment me, to keep me from being too elated. Three times I appealed to the Lord about this, that it would leave me, but he said to me, "My grace is sufficient for you, for power is made perfect in weakness." (2 Cor. 12:7–9)

> But we have this treasure in clay jars, so that it may be made clear that this extraordinary power belongs to God and does not come from us. We are afflicted in every way but not crushed; perplexed, but not driven to despair; persecuted, but not forsaken; struck down, but not destroyed; always carrying in the body the death of Jesus, so that the life of Jesus may also be made visible in our bodies. (2 Cor. 4:7–10)

Throughout Scripture we find the theme that God's purposes and power work through people with weaknesses. Moses claims he does not speak well. Amos is from the wrong side of town. Jeremiah is way too young. The suffering servant of Isaiah is unsightly and abused, yet he becomes a beacon of salvation to the nations. Jesus dies in weakness and agony on the cross, yet through his resurrection God's power is made manifest to the world (1 Cor. 1:27; Rom 8:26; Heb. 5:2; 7:18; 13:04).

Pastoral Shoots: Potential Damage to Listeners' Lives

God's power is manifest in human weakness and suffering. God is available to help us learn valuable lessons from our hardships. Making those claims is different from preaching that God causes suffering. To attribute illness and death and betrayal and earthquakes and drive-by shootings to the hand of God can only serve to make people feel bad about themselves or bad about God. Such preaching causes listeners to sink into guilt, or it stirs up anger within them at God.

This attribution of suffering to God raises more questions than it answers: Why aren't some blatantly sinful people visited with suffering? Why are all not tested by misfortune at the hand of God? Doesn't everyone deserve this coveted opportunity for faith growth? Why does God need to manifest divine power? Is God insecure or egotistical? If someone's life doesn't have much suffering, what do we make of that? Are experiences of suffering and pain inherently good? If so, is it easier for a masochist to be a good disciple than for the rest of us?

What about the inconsistencies among these messages about God? Say that one week I preach that God wants abundance (defined as health, prosperity, etc.) for you. I tell you that you need to have more faith. I tell you that if you think positive, faith-filled thoughts, these negative conditions will disappear from your life.

Then the next week I tell you that your sufferings are God testing you to strengthen you (what my dad used to call "very well disguised blessings"). That would mean you wouldn't be caught dead without your misfortunes, illnesses, and tragedies, right? Saying that God brings abundance (understood in superficial terms) and that God brings suffering is problematic on several counts. It does God an injustice, it fosters guilt and self-loathing, and it contains logical inconsistencies that make it unbelievably confusing. Add to that that it cannot be supported by the whole canon, with which we are supposed to be in an interactive dialogue as interpreters of God's word for God's people.

The book of Job contests the whole notion that suffering is God's punishment for sin, since Job is an innocent, righteous man. God condemns the charges of Job's friends at the end of the book. The book never answers the question of why the righteous suffer. Instead, it affirms the complexity of the cosmos and the transcendence of a mysterious God that make knowing the answer beyond current human capacities. At the same time, the book affirms the certainty of the divine presence in human suffering.

Jesus counters this notion that suffering is God's punishment for sin in Luke 13:1–5. He refers to Galileans killed by Pilate and righteous people killed when the tower of Siloam fell on them. He challenges the notion that these events befell the victims because they were worse sinners than anyone else.

What to Say about God

I'm not just interested in demolition. I'm also interested in construction. There certainly are constructs I want to help build in listeners' minds about the character of God, things I definitely want to affirm about God repeatedly in my sermons. Three come immediately to mind.

God's Ultimate Purposes Will Be Achieved, Despite All Obstacles

Divine purposes shape and reshape history and, in the end, will not be thwarted. A common affirmation in African American sermons is "God can do anything but fail." God intends to and will bring about the fulfillment or realization of creation (Hodgson and King 1982, 92). That may be a hard sell these days, given the violence and disarray of the world in which we live. When we preach God's larger redemptive purpose for creation, people may respond, "That's great, but what matters to me is the purpose of my life. Rick Warren says I'm to live a 'purpose-driven life,' but I've hit a speed bump. What does it matter if God's wide-angle lens shows a picture of redemption and joy when my zoom lens shows a picture of illness and loss?"

It's more important than ever to preach that God's good intentions will be achieved for humankind and the world. The resurrection is testimony to the fact that human disobedience and brutality cannot kill God's life and purpose.

When John Wesley thought about God as Sovereign, he focused not so much on God as a controlling power but on God as a loving parent and the giver of the gift of human freewill. He insisted that God's sovereignty never be considered in isolation from God's other attributes, in abstraction from God's justice and love. He believed that the biblical notion of the "glory of God" does not refer primarily to God's power, but to the manifestation of all God's attributes, especially justice and love. He believed that our sovereign God gives human freewill as a gift. God continually issues the divine invitation to sinful human beings to respond to God's unmerited gracious forgiveness. Human beings have the freewill to resist God's initiatives, but not to call a halt to God's Grace, which forgives us and then invites and empowers us to respond to that invitation (Maddox 1994, 54–55).

Preachers need to key in to the contrast between people's pain and the promise that God has an overarching purpose. To say, "God's loving purpose trumps your painful present!" is not enough. We should never underestimate the depth and seriousness of the unspoken theological questions people bring with them to church on Sundays (Wood 2008, ix). "What to say about God" cannot be handled in a summer sermon series, even if it's reproduced on the church Web site for those who were on vacation. It is the substance of every sermon. It deserves the lifelong attention of the preacher, her best theological thinking, her best efforts to present what we know about the character and workings of God in a manner that is clear yet nuanced—a tall order.

This means the preacher will have to talk about the doctrine of providence, for this has been the way Christian theology has addressed the issue of how God relates to the world God has created. It addresses the question "How am I to understand what is going on in relation to God, and how am I to understand God in relation to what is going on?" Traditional Western theology tends to portray a universal order in which everything that happens is specifically arranged by God to serve God's good purposes. This understanding tends to divorce the doctrine of providence from the fullness of the Trinity, emphasizing God's relation to human events in terms of control (Wood 2008, 16). In his book *The Question of Providence*, theologian Charles Wood points out that there is a difference between the traditional Western notion of providence, that "God is providing everything that goes on," and the understanding he prefers: "In everything that goes on, God is providing" (Wood 2008, 73).

Instead of traditional depictions of God's sovereignty as equating everything that happens with the will of God, we can preach that God provides in everything that goes on, as a triune community, empowering creaturely existence and action, allowing creaturely conflict and failing, opposing the consequences of creaturely failures and mistakes, and working in and with each situation toward new possibilities for the fulfillment of creation's purposes. God orders creaturely activities toward God's own purposes (Wood 2008, 90).

Incorporating people's questions, confusion, pain, and doubt into my sermons, I will continue to preach the goodness and ultimate unthwartability of the plans of God our Creator, Sustainer, and Redeemer. Our daily lives are a response to this God—what Jesus referred to as entering into the kingdom of God, which is already and yet to be. Our daily lives have purpose individually and as the body of Christ. Rabbinic theology contains a beautiful definition of the purpose of our lives lived in response to this sovereign God: Our lives are to be a participation in *tikkun olam* (the repair of the world). The traditional Jewish "Aleinu," a prayer said three times a day in some Jewish traditions, affirms that our acts of religious obligation are to perfect the world under the sovereignty of God.

God Is a Steadfast Presence with Us in Our Suffering

God's Grace can bring growth and redemption out of our suffering. When we turn to God in our suffering, we may find that we grow in our faith and that we learn valuable lessons that flow out to touch the lives of those around us.

We may experience God's power in our own weakness. To say that God brings this effect from our suffering is not to say God caused our suffering in order to bring about that effect. Leslie Weatherhead, a prominent Methodist preacher in London during World War II, authored a now-famous little book called *The Will of God*. In it he spoke of the "intentional will of God" (God's original intentions for joy and justice in all human circumstances), "the circumstantial will of God" (the good God can do from human sin in bad circumstances), and "the ultimate will of God" (the unthwartable, ultimate accomplishment of God's intentions for joy and justice in all human circumstances).

To ascribe suffering to the hand of God so that people might be disciplined and God's power might be made palpable is to confuse the circumstantial will of God with the intentional will of God.

A pastor was in a hospital in Denver, Colorado, comforting a friend of his whose son was dying of a rare disease. Over coffee in the hospital cafeteria the friend said, "You know, this may sound odd. But the best theological statement I can think of to fit this situation is that 'Stuff happens' and God doesn't cause the stuff." The friend used a version of "stuff" that would not be appropriate in the pulpit, but he got his point across.

Recently in a community near where I live, four Jehovah's Witnesses were killed in a car accident on their way to worship. A reporter asked a friend from their church, "How do you deal with something like this?" The friend said, "There is such a thing as being in the wrong place at the wrong time. And it can happen, no matter how deep someone's faith is, and is no judgment on that faith."

In the suffering of daily life, God is present with the sufferers—not passively present, but powerfully so—and is able to bring redemptive results from excruciating experiences. By our compassion for those who suffer and our opposition to systemic injustice, we embody God's presence and are ourselves agents of divine redemption in others' suffering.

God Is the Source of Our Abundance at the Deepest Level

In my warnings about the prosperity gospel, I don't want to throw the baby out with the bathwater. God gives great and glorious gifts to those who open their lives to God's presence and purpose. I'd suggest that any preacher of the Gospel (as distinguished from the prosperity gospel) read Scripture with an eye for the gifts God has on offer for those with the sense to seek them. I'd suggest we preach about them and invite people to recognize, enjoy, and share them.

John Wesley, paraphrasing 1 Corinthians 4:7, asked himself more than once in his life, "What have I that I have not received?" Scripture contains myriad affirmations of the good gifts of God:

> [Wisdom] is more precious than jewels, and nothing you desire can compare with her. (Prov. 3:15)

> I have come that they may have life and have it abundantly." (John 10:10)

> Bless the Lord, O my soul, and do not forget all his benefits." (Ps. 103:2; the psalmist goes on to talk about forgiveness, sustenance, and renewed zeal for following God)

> For us there is one God, the Father, from whom are all things and for whom we exist. (1 Cor. 8:6)

> The fruit of the Spirit is love, joy, peace, patience, kindness, generosity, faithfulness, gentleness, and self-control. (Gal. 5:22–23)

I want my sermons to be the building blocks of those three sturdy theological assurances: that God's purpose for the redemption of our world will not be thwarted, that God is proactively present with us in situations that seem to belie that assurance, and that everything we have and are is a gift from God.

It's important in preaching to be as clear about what we are not saying as we are about what we are saying. To that end, note three things. First, affirming the sovereignty of God is not the same as insisting that everything that happens in my life and the world is directly the result of God's actions. Second, affirming God's presence with us to bring about redemptive results from suffering is not the same as saying God sent them for that purpose. Third, affirming that everything we have and are is a gift from God is not the same as believing in the prosperity gospel—that my good health, my financial prosperity, and my promotion at work are the signs of God's favor to me for my faith and positive prayers and that, conversely, my declining health and finances are signs of God's disfavor.

The pastoral implications of these positive affirmations about God have tremendous healing power. Since God doesn't dole out suffering as punishment for our sin, then the presence of suffering doesn't signal the absence of God and a deepening of our guilt and self-loathing. If God doesn't dole out suffering to teach and discipline us, suffering doesn't have to lead to resentment toward God. If God doesn't dole out suffering so that divine power can be showcased, then we will be more likely to call on that power when sorrows sap our strength. If God doesn't dole out wealth and health and good fortune as a reward for our positive thoughts or righteous living, then we can stop feeling at fault when we suffer the kind of setbacks that are inevitable in every life. When we enjoy career advancement or good fortune, we can relinquish our sense of self-congratulation. If God helps us to accomplish a worthwhile goal, we can offer God thanks and gratitude and echo the apostle Paul and John Wesley: "What have I that I have not received from the hand of God?"

Since God is a God of purpose, compassion, and gracious generosity, we can say so in every sermon, with conviction, creativity, and clarity.

I've sung alto in the church choir for years. My all-time favorite anthem is called "Write Your Blessed Name." The melody is haunting, and the words, based on a poem by Thomas à Kempis (1380–1471), are more eloquent an ending to this chapter than any I could devise:

> Write your blessed name, O Lord, upon my heart.
> There to remain, so indelibly engraved
> That no prosperity, no adversity
> Ever move me from thy love.

Questions for Reflection

1. Have I told people that what happens to them is from the hand of God?
2. Have I told them God is the source of their material abundance?
3. Have I implied that those who are materially comfortable are more favored by God than those who are not?
4. Have I told them that God is the cause of their suffering?
5. Have I told them God sends suffering to punish them? To teach them? So God's power can be manifest in their misery and weakness?
6. Have I implied that when they suffer, God is pleased?
7. Have I implied that their pain is intrinsically a good thing?
8. Have I said anything that would impel a person in an abusive relationship to stay in it to please God?
9. Have I affirmed that God has a gracious purpose for the redemption of the world, of which our lives are a part?
10. Have I affirmed that God is a steadfast and empowering presence in suffering?
11. Have I affirmed that God is the source of all spiritual blessings in our lives?

Chapter 2

What Not to Say (and What to Say) about the Bible

The trouble is the Bible is not like any other book. To read the Bible as literature is like reading Moby Dick *as a whaling manual or* The Brothers Karamazov *for its punctuation.*
                    Frederick Buechner, Wishful Thinking

The inspiration of the Bible depends upon the ignorance of the gentleman who reads it.
                    R. G. Ingersoll, "Speech" (1881)

Explanations are often exotic
And maintained with a fierceness despotic.
Sollie's Song deals with God?
And the church? My, how odd.
To me it seems merely erotic.

                                        Isaac Asimov

*T*his chapter really does go "where angels fear to tread." The Bible is the most-bought, least-read, most-abused, most-loved, most-contentious, most-likely-to-be-used-as-a-weapon volume in all of recorded history. The three quotations I have chosen to head the chapter (from the many billions of bon mots I might have chosen) point to the white caps of these troubled waters. Buechner warns that the Bible is far more than merely literature, though he would surely agree that some of it clearly is precisely that (Jonah and Ruth, among others?). Ingersoll warns in his droll aphorism that when it comes to reading the Bible, one person's inspiration may be another's inanity. And this observation is emphasized by Asimov's clever and sophisticated limerick; the Song of Songs, traditionally attributed to King Solomon, has historically been read as an allegory, dealing in fact with God (though God is not mentioned at all) or with the church (neither is anything like

20

a church or synagogue cited). He finds it "merely erotic," as have many commentators.

So what's a preacher to do with this glorious conglomeration of history, theology, psychology, pseudoscience, poetry, narrative, proverb, parable, war, death, wrath (human and divine), unfailing love (less human, more divine), mystery, liturgy, and more? I admit at times to a certain envy for some of our Unitarian Universalist students who take the Bible as one book among many and often find Emerson or Thoreau much more to their homiletical liking. But we more traditional Christians (and both of the authors of this book are among the "mainest" of the mainline) agree with Buechner: The Bible really is somehow more than merely literature, more than merely just another book. It is primarily the church's and the synagogue's book, having birthed the church and synagogue, sustained the church and synagogue, challenged the church and synagogue, puzzled the church and synagogue, and promised the church and synagogue a future. In addition to that, it rests as bedrock of whatever might be called Western civilization, its laws, its tussles over the proper relationship between church and state, its attempts to order a society where all its members have access to "life, liberty, and the pursuit of happiness," to quote one famous series of words steeped in the language and cadences of the Bible. For the Christian preacher, a homiletical conversation with the Bible offers the final subject of all preaching: the presence and purposes of God in the cosmos. Without the ancient text, we have no one place to begin our discussion of that most basic concern.

What Not to Say about the Bible

The Bible Is a Book of Answers

When preachers suggest that the Bible offers answers "to life's persistent questions" (quoting Garrison Keillor's alter ego Guy Noir), they in effect say that the Bible is some sort of textbook for soul tune-ups or a self-help book for confused people, a Cliffs Notes summary of proper living. This, of course, is not to say that certain kinds of answers cannot be gleaned from the ancient pages of the Bible; too often, however, characterizing the Bible as an answer book is to reduce it to a conversation stopper at best or a bludgeon against one's enemies at worst. Try the following examples.

Example 1

In a sermon titled "What Does the Bible Say about Getting Even?" the preacher chooses Psalm 137 as the text. This psalm begins with the deep sorrow of exile and its challenges to keep faith in God in a foreign land, but it ends with a powerful demand that God take the infant children of certain allies of the conquering Babylonians and bash them against rocks. It is a clear call for getting even. Psalm 109 is then noted to strengthen the point that the Bible says that it is okay to get even. The sermon adds a reference to Exodus 21:25 with its famous "eye for an eye, tooth for a tooth" declaration, and then it moves to an ancient song in Genesis 4:24 in which Lamech clamors for "seventy times seven" vengeance against anyone who has the temerity to assault him. The sermon concludes with Jesus' words to Peter that he must forgive any who sin against him "seventy times seven." Thus, the biblical answer to the question of getting even is no; one should be like Jesus who demanded near-infinite forgiveness. Next question?

This will not do as a biblical "answer" concerning vengeance. That is so for many reasons, three of which I will discuss here. First, it implies that the Old Testament is characterized only as a book filled with calls for vengeance. This is a false claim, as a reading of Hosea 11, Jeremiah 8–9, Isaiah 52–53, among many other passages makes clear. Second, it implies further that Jesus rejected the supposed Old Testament belief just shown to be false and always called his followers to forgive. But that is not true either. Jesus on occasion was harsh with his opponents, calling some of them "those who devour widows' houses and make long, false prayers" (Luke 20:47) and urging his disciples to "shake off the dust from your feet" of places that did not welcome them, saying those places will fare worse than Sodom and Gomorrah "on the day of judgment" (Matt. 10:14–15). Third, the Bible is less concerned about vengeance than it is concerned about justice, the redressing of inequity. There is little doubt that talk of justice can lead to brutality when one person's justice is achieved at the expense of someone else's rights. But the simple sermon on "getting even" has in fact offered an "answer" that is not at all what the Bible tries to say about this very complex human social problem.

The difficulty of any social problem does not mean that we should not turn to the Bible for help in addressing such issues, but it warns that biblical "answers" are not reached by quoting a few isolated verses that cover a thousand years of writing and reflection on such issues.

Example 2

I am often asked to address "what the Bible says about . . ." Many sorts of questions provoke this interest: war and peace, parenting, sexuality, family, worship, music, to name only a few. Again, the preacher must use extreme caution when approaching such twenty-first-century concerns with the aid of a very ancient book, one written over at least a thousand years, in social contexts thoroughly distinct from our own, and in languages we no longer speak. I listened to a sermon once titled "Why Gay Is Not Okay." The preacher quoted the seven biblical references that are regularly used to exclude gay and lesbian persons from full acceptance in church and in modern society. The concluding discussion of the sermon referred to statements in Paul's letter to the Christians in Rome where the apostle chides some people, unnamed in the letter, who have "exchanged the truth about God for a lie." As a result, Paul says that "God gave them up to degrading passions." His examples are that "their women exchanged natural intercourse for unnatural," while the men, "giving up natural intercourse with women, were consumed with passion for one another" (Rom. 1:26–27). The preacher concluded that homosexuality is unacceptable for a Christian, because Paul condemned it.

What are the problems with this "answer" sermon? First, Paul was writing nearly two thousand years ago. His understanding of human sexual behavior was limited to what was considered "natural" at the time, namely, heterosexual relationships. Thus, he believed, as did many of his time, that there could be no such thing as a committed homosexual relationship, one built squarely on love. There were certainly such relationships in Paul's day, but by his understanding those relationships were "unnatural." I know committed homosexual persons whose relationships are based on love and mutuality. Why then should I judge such relationships "unnatural," based on one view of what is natural, expressed two thousand years ago? I am not a fundamentalist; I do not judge Paul's sometimes exclusive views of women's roles in community as "natural" for all time (1 Cor. 11). Why should I think so about homosexual relationships?

The second problem with this sermon is that Paul's condemnation of these so-called "debased minds" (1:28), noteworthy for their "degrading passions," does not conclude with sexual activity: "They were filled with every kind of wickedness, evil, covetousness, malice. Full of envy, murder, strife, deceit, craftiness, they are gossips, slanderers, God-haters, insolent, haughty, boastful, inventors of evil, rebellious toward parents, foolish, faithless, heartless, ruthless." Whew! That list could be said to include just about every imaginable nasty thing that humans can conceive. If I am to conclude that same-sex relationships are somehow disallowed by God, then why am I not as intent on rooting out these other, apparently equally dangerous human traits? Why do I not expend energy to shine a spotlight on these behaviors and exclude all those who exhibit them? The result, of course, would be empty churches and empty pulpits!

Finally, the Bible is not primarily concerned with sexual relationships but with justice among the nations, the appropriate use of money, and the proper love of neighbor, along with the proper identification of just who that neighbor is.

This so-called "answer" to a question is little better than the rawest kind of proof-texting, where a few verses, written over many hundreds of years, from several different contexts, are cobbled together as an "answer" to an issue that has presented itself uniquely to our culture. Such "answers" are false to the rich and complex contexts that the ancient text represents. Both of these example sermons demonstrate how the Bible is far more than a book providing simple answers to simple questions.

Quoting the Bible a Lot Does Not a Biblical Sermon Make

When committees searching for new preachers are asked what they want, the answer almost invariably is, "We want a biblical preacher." By that they appear to mean that they want someone who knows what is in the Bible, who loves what is in it, and who is ready and able to express what is in it with passion and energy. But I think there is in fact very little agreement about what precisely that demand means. Let us take each part of the sentence in turn.

What Is in the Bible

One would think that since we can all go to any number of stores and buy a Bible, open its covers, and read it, we could agree on the main points of what is being said therein. Of course, we would be wrong! The proof of how wrong we would be may be found in the existence of over 1,500 Protestant denominations in the United States alone. Each of them, to a lesser or greater extent, came to be because of some contentious reading of what is "really" in the Bible. When the members of our pulpit committee want a preacher who knows "what is in the Bible," they need to ask several follow-up questions: What is the Bible's central concern? What is the relationship between the Old and New Testaments? Just what sort of book is the Bible anyway? How is it the word of God? You may think of many more, I am sure. The point is obvious: Knowing what is in the Bible may or may not have any real relationship to its significance for the members in the church. It is quite conceivable that one could have the entire Bible memorized in several older or newer translations and know very little about the Bible at all. To be able to quote the Bible is no sign of a genuine knowledge of "what is in it."

A Love of What Is in It

I genuinely love what is in the Bible, but I have spoken to many persons in my ministerial life who are just as convinced that I hate the Bible. Why is this so? My understanding of what is in the Bible does not match what their understanding is; hence, what I love about my understanding of what is in it does not match their love of their understanding of what is in it. For example, I love the constant challenge that much of the Bible raises against my selfish individualism, my refusal to "hear the cry of the needy." Others hear such emphases as tantamount to liberal social control, insisting that the Bible is about their individual relationship to Jesus and his suffering and death for their individual salvation and promise of heaven. I plainly hear something they do not, while they emphasize something I hear but think has been misused.

Passion and Energy for Its Proclamation

Because we do not agree on what is in the Bible, and hence place our love of what is in it in different places, my passion and energy may not be gladly received by those who wish that proclamation were placed in the service of what they think is in it, rather than what I think is in it.

The quest for a "biblical preacher" is indeed a complex quest. Merely quoting the Bible a lot in your preaching does not necessarily make you a biblical preacher. All preachers who use the Bible regularly in their preaching need to think long and hard about what they think is actually in the Bible, how they love what is in it (and perhaps love less some of the stuff in it), and how they are anxious to preach what they love with energy and passion.

The Bible's Meaning Is Not Very Important Apart from the Lives of Our Hearers

The Bible is not a magical book whose simple opening can aromatically transform sinners to saints. The fact that I have an address from which I can purchase the entire Bible on a microchip, however, lets me know that the idea that the Bible really is magic is abroad in the land. Martin Marty calls the Bible an icon in our culture, a sort of talisman that mystically wards off evil and potentially makes us better—even if we do not read it well or much! An old colleague of mine loved to say that he never met a Methodist who did not want to want to study the Bible. But even if we do decide to study it, and fairly seriously, what good is it to know that there are two creation stories in the first two chapters of Genesis? That there are two accounts of the flood in Genesis 6–8 ("two-by-two" in 6:19 and "seven pairs" in 7:2)? That Moses was placed in an "ark" to float on the Nile, not a basket? These bits of Bible information are interesting; they could well be used to wow your Christian friends or to stop a conversation at coffee hour. I can study the Bible apart from its impact for me, but if I do only that, I reduce its value to trivia. I am prepared to go on *Jeopardy* and hope for the category "Bible," but the point of my study of the Bible at all will soon be lost, no matter how much money I might win.

Preachers preach from the Bible because they try to hear in their chosen text a word for us, for them and their hearers. How all of us, preachers and hearers, find ourselves to be at this particular moment profoundly determines just how the preacher preaches and how the hearer hears. If preachers are not attentive to the specific context of their preparation for preaching and the specific context of the preaching itself, they are doing little more than offering general Bible trivia, occasionally interesting, sometimes thought-provoking, but seldom transforming.

Example 1

I once heard a student sermon that began, "Did you know that Paul uses the word "law," *nomos* in Greek, in six different ways in the third chapter of Romans?" The students in the class silently groaned when they heard that, because the promise of this beginning was that we were all in for a lengthy time of it. We were not disappointed—about the length, that is. After the preacher had turned to the third way in which Paul uses the word "law" in Romans 3, some eight or nine minutes into what was to have been a fifteen-minute sermon, and after perusing the glazing eyes before him, he suddenly stopped and said, "Is this as boring to you as it is to me?" Of course, we all laughed uproariously. Part of our laughter was that we had in fact been bored out of our skulls, but another part was the gracious fact that we had been released from the other meanings of the word "law" in Romans 3. Though it may be interesting to know the details of Paul's vocabulary—and serious preachers do spend time worrying about such things when we preach sermons on Paul—as preachers our job is finally not to help our hearers understand Paul better, but to do what Paul was trying to do, namely, proclaim the Gospel of Jesus to people in desperate need of hearing it.

It may be that my knowledge about Paul and the law will be crucial for my presentation of the Gospel for that day, but such knowledge can never be an end in itself. I am not transformed in the light of the Gospel by knowing what Paul meant by "law." The context of my preparation of the sermon, and the context of my preaching of it, will go a long way toward determining just how I will use this information about Paul and the law.

I always ask my students to use their fellow students and me as the congregation to which they have been called to preach. We are all in seminary, sharing the same space and many of the same concerns, stresses, and hopes. I had hoped that my student would have helped us see that Paul is up to something quite radical in Romans 3. He is claiming that in Christ, the old distinction of Jew and Gentile, a distinction for "who is in and who is out," has been erased in the "righteousness of God through the faith of Jesus" (or "through faith in Jesus," a notorious ambiguity). What might this mean for those of us in the class—for me as the teacher, the one who has power by virtue of his position on the faculty, and for those who are students, some supremely gifted for ministry, some less so, some fully certain of a call from God, some still struggling with that call? How can this word of "no distinction" be heard by each one of us? And what does Paul's multilayered understanding of "law" have to do with it? By dwelling only on vocabulary, my student deprived us of the life-giving power that Paul was pointing to by his detailed speech. That speech to the Romans was not finally about law; it was about what Christ had done for Paul and for them. Ron Allen frames the problem well: "The test of the expository sermon is not the question, 'Did the pastor preach the text?' . . . The better test is, 'Did the pastor preach the Gospel through the community's encounter with the text?'" (Allen, *Interpreting the Gospel*, 103)

Example 2

In chapter 3, I use as an example a sermon I preached on Exodus 32 that I called "Will the Real Leader Please Stand Up?" I suggest that the sermon was a pure story sermon, one that uses a retelling of the Bible story alone to make its claims. I want here to suggest just how dangerous—because it is so much fun—such a sermon can be. Here's how I began: "Moses dripped sweat as he stumbled down the mountain. It had been exhausting talking with God." I think this is a gripping start and that most hearers would be attentive to the story to follow. There is a danger, however, of enjoying the story so much that you forget just why you are telling it. If I get caught up in the details of the sweat, dust, lewd dancing, grinding up of the molten calf, and so forth, I run the risk of entertainment for entertainment's sake, rather than allowing the story to make its own particular claims. This is especially hazardous for those who love stories and love to tell them with drama and energy.

I watched an old sermon recently on YouTube entitled "Pay Day, Someday." Its nearly fifty-five-minute length was a retelling of the story of Naboth's vineyard in 1 Kings 21. The preacher, a Rev. Lee, used a keen imagination in his telling, and he kept the listener apprised that the reason he was using the story was to warn us that there would be a payday someday. Ahab's perfidious behavior brought about his downfall, as predicted by Elijah the prophet. Jezebel's lies and judicial murder of Naboth brought about her horrible death in the jaws of some "filthy, mangy, stray dogs," as predicted by Elijah the prophet. And the sermon ended with the stark warning that those who do not receive Jesus as savior will end as the royal pair did, because "there always is a payday someday."

This long sermon was in effect a "shaggy dog" story. It made its one terrifying point at the end of a very lengthy tale from the Hebrew Bible whose claims had nothing to do with the acceptance or nonacceptance of Jesus. I was indeed caught up in the telling, though some of it was quite disgusting in its gruesome details, but the reason for the telling was forced and false to what I had been hearing. I have no doubt that the hearers gave their attention to the story—Rev. Lee claimed to have preached this same sermon over a thousand times!—but the story was something like a red herring, planted in the sermon as a trick to get to an old Gospel demand. Frankly, at the end I felt fooled, swindled into listening to that old command "to be saved" before it is too late. Of course, this may certainly be the message that Rev. Lee's original audiences expected to hear. But new technology has moved his preaching into a far broader arena of listeners, robbing it of whatever context it once had and adding many newer unanticipated twenty-first-century contexts. Naboth's sad and terrible story of injustice and murder—and a great story it is—has lost its unique theological significance by being shoehorned onto another foot entirely.

Example 3

There is at least one more danger in rich retellings of stories from the Bible. The preacher can get the impression that the story itself is enough, that she does not have to work hard to keep the point of the story for this day alive for the hearer. There is little doubt that many of the Bible's stories are masterfully written. There is nothing quite like them in the literature of the ancient world. I have often said that the complex portraits of David and Saul are unmatched until the time of Shakespeare, over two thousand years later. But that very complexity makes it doubly important that the preacher make crystal clear to the congregation just how she has heard this part of the story for this day, how she has heard it for us today. Without that clarity, it remains just a grand story, like *Great Expectations* or *Hamlet* or *Jane Eyre*. But the Bible is more; it is somehow the word of God for us and must be preached as such. After hearing about David or Saul, I ask myself what transformational word I have experienced for this day. Without that question, preaching becomes merely fun, a pleasant way to spend a Sunday morning in a cool and dry place.

Do Not Get Stuck in Your Favorite Part of the Bible

Marcion, a second-century bishop of the early church, had a novel approach to Scripture. He determined that all that Jewish stuff was dangerous and confusing, so he commanded that all things Jewish should be expunged from the Bible. That included, of course, all the Old Testament and whatever Marcion decided was Jewish in the New Testament. He was not left with much! By some accounts (we have none of Marcion's own writings), he kept only part of the Gospel of Luke and four letters of Paul. Those bleeding chunks composed the bishop's Bible. Some years after his death he was judged a heretic for such thoughts. The church decided by the fourth century that the Bible was finally something like the one you and I can purchase and read today.

But the joke may be on the church, and wherever Marcion is spending his eternity, a smile may regularly cross his face. For in the pulpits of the twenty-first century, little is heard from the Old Testament, save Isaiah at Christmas and Easter, and the Jewish portions of the New Testament are too often used as evil foils for the "right-thinking" Jesus, who came along to save us from all that Jewish stuff. I caricature, but not much. In short, too many preachers spend too much time in their "favorites" and relegate vast swatches of the Bible to an undeserved oblivion. It has been said that over 75 percent of sermons from Christian pulpits today say little or nothing about the Hebrew Bible. And, as we have seen, what is said is too often caricatured as a "whipping boy" for the "vastly superior" words and wisdom of Jesus and Paul. To treat the Bible in such a fashion is to misrepresent it very dangerously. At the end of the day, the church is the church because of the whole Bible, not just the New Testament and Psalms.

What to Say about the Bible

The Bible is the bedrock of the church's life and witness. To do church without the Bible is like playing football without the ball; those on the field have no notion of where they are, what they are to do, or what the point of the game is at all. We preachers begin with the Bible because those particular ancient words enable us to do some very basic and crucial tasks, tasks that always are under threat by the siren sounds of being "up to date."

God Is the Subject of Our Preaching

In a time when the fastest-growing "religious" group in the United States is nonbelievers, it is more than ever important to remind ourselves and our hearers that the cosmos in which we live is not finally left to move or evolve merely in random ways; it is shot through with a power not our own. Though so-called liberals and so-called conservatives (finally not very illuminating terms) may speak somewhat differently about this power, Christians have long called it God. And in the pages of the Bible is where this God is most certainly named and addressed and heard. The Bible helps us to focus our preaching squarely on God, who is finally the subject of all our preaching. Every sermon we preach is about what God has done, is doing, and will do for us and our cosmos, and not primarily about what we have done, are doing, or will do, though the latter ought fall directly from the former, and in that order. Too many sermons I hear are less about God and more about us—what we ought to do, how we ought to think, what we ought to say. The Bible teaches us what God is doing, hoping, speaking, urging, luring, cajoling. Sermons that end always with "Go, thou, and do likewise" must be grounded in the truth of what God has done and said that leads us to go and do likewise.

Returning to Exodus 32, it is very easy to focus the sermon's attention on the astonishing dialogue between Moses and God, especially at the courage of Moses in confronting the Almighty One, whose anger at the evils of the people seems terrifyingly out of control. Yet it cannot be forgotten that God not only listens to Moses' arguments on behalf of his wayward people, but finally changes the divine mind as a result of those arguments. What better example can one find that God invites our prayers and hopes and even our demands and is in partnership with us on our journey toward the future? Moses is certainly the model of real leadership in the story, but without a God who listens and reacts, there is no story of Israel's future at all. Some rabbis have surmised that when God demanded Moses "to get out of my way," what God meant in part was an invitation to Moses to respond rather than meekly acquiesce.

We Need to Recover the Language of the Bible

Preaching from the Bible can aid the church in its recovery of biblical language. If the Bible really is the foundation of the church's life, and I claim that it is, its words have suffered serious abuse over the past few generations. That abuse has come in several guises.

Its words have been used to support more than a few reprehensible causes and beliefs. From the racist rants of the Ku Klux Klan, to the fiery demands of wild-eyed, would-be messiahs (Jim Jones to David Koresh), to murderous anti-abortionists, to women who murder their own babies, claiming direction by the Scripture, the Bible's words have been portrayed as prescriptions for mayhem and slaughter. These very public uses of the Bible have generated deep antagonism toward the book and made many wonder just what sort of material may be found there. For some, it has become impossible any longer to find value in such a thing at all. Even serious believers question the role of the Bible in our time. Could it be that its antiquity, its creation in a very different time from our own, its odd customs and quaint ideas are increasingly problematic for a grown-up scientific age? The only way to address these serious questions and concerns is to get back into the language of the texts and allow modern hearers to experience their relevance and crucial importance even now.

Not only have cruel uses been made of the Bible's language, but seemingly pleasant and pleasurable implications have been found in the Bible's words. "Have a better attitude, and life will be good," coo some preachers, waving a Bible in front of their many listeners. "Believe correctly and you will prosper," shout others in their Saville Row suits, behind their Plexiglas pulpits, having stepped from their fully equipped luxury cars. "David was a great sinner, and so are you, but no matter! God has chosen you to be great, and that is all that counts," teach those who find ways to excuse very public strayings by very public and very powerful people. When the Bible is used in these ways, its serious demands for lives transformed rather than conformed to this world are forgotten in the rush to find support for a life we already love to live and do not want confronted by the sharp demands of justice and righteousness for all of God's people.

Narrow issues of the culture become the only thing that counts, and the richer and fuller resources of the Bible are forgotten. A recent meeting of the Evangelical Theological Society makes the point. Those gathered spent an entire day excoriating gays and lesbians and quoting the six or seven verses from the Bible that seem to support their exclusion. On the second day, one man stood up, holding a copy of the Bible in each hand. He said, "In my left hand I am holding a Bible from which I have cut all the verses that address the issue of homosexuality. In my right I hold a Bible from which I have cut all the verses that address the issue of the right and wrong uses of money." The first Bible appeared to be nearly intact, while the second one was in tatters, riddled with hundreds of excisions. "Which one of these Bibles suggests what is of the more crucial significance?" he asked. He was not implying that homosexuality was not an important issue, but he was saying that the Bible's concern for the right use of resources seemed to be of greater moment. Perhaps he was saying too that we have missed crucial words in the Bible that could serve us well as we grapple with many large issues of the twenty-first century.

To use the Bible rightly is to be acquainted with its multiple concerns, its broad and complex treatment of many issues. I have a test for you. If when you read a text from the Bible and do not immediately think of five other texts in the Bible that address the issues of that first text, you do not know your Bible well enough and you run the risk of proof-texting, pulling from the Bible one or two juicy bits to support or to deny one thing or another. I hasten to add that proof-texting is a game played by so-called liberals and conservatives. This will not do. Your hearers should expect better from you, and you should expect better from yourself.

The Bible Offers Central Expressions for Our Emerging Faith

Surely much of the vast confusion concerning just what the Christian faith is in the twenty-first century may be traced to the vast ignorance of what is in the Bible. It is commonly, and foolishly, said, "You can prove anything from the Bible." This absurd claim is patently not true, but it has become a truism due to biblical ignorance and misuse. Any preacher must remember the very first thing learned in seminary: The Bible was not written by one person on the same day. Its pages represent over a thousand years of reflection on the central questions of God, Christ, the Spirit, Grace, righteousness, sin, forgiveness—those issues and ideas that make up the core of the faith. Because this is true, no single statement concerning the Bible's content ought to begin, "The Bible says . . ."

If I choose a text like Genesis 1 as the basis for a sermon on God, I run the risk of claiming that now that I have worked with that one text, I have plumbed the Bible's central concern about the One we have assembled to worship. It is important to focus like a laser beam on that one text for this one sermon, but I must never imply that with that one text the subject has now been fully presented, that this is what the Bible says. Such a claim is dangerous nonsense! What about Genesis 2 or Exodus 32 or Jeremiah 20 or Psalm 137 or Job 38 or Mark 16 or James 2? The Bible's claims for God, its groping to understand the creator of the heavens and the earth, match the struggles of the congregation that has come to hear the sermon. As the congregation and the preacher labor together toward a fuller understanding of the Divine One, the sermon must never imply that the Bible says only one thing about its central professions.

Every preacher is responsible in her congregation to be "the Bible expert." Others know more about parking lots and boilers and certificates of deposit, but the preacher is expected to know the Bible. Hence, spend time in its pages and study it assiduously, faithfully, carefully, constantly. Only then will you be a biblical preacher, and only then will the church be nourished by the living word of the Bible.

The Preacher Should Nurture a Rich Biblical Imagination

One of the skills that a preacher of the Bible simply must cultivate is the use of the grand organ imagination that God has given to each of us. I call imagination an organ in the multiple meanings of that word. The organ of imagination can be seen as another part of the body designed for some specific task: Just as the heart pumps blood, so our imaginations envision what is not there and create new ideas. But imaginations are also like musical organs, great collections of pipes that, when playing together, create new worlds of sound, crashingly loud and whisperingly soft, piercingly demanding and achingly inviting.

Unfortunately, too much of our education has rendered our imaginations dull, if not mute. "Just the facts, ma'am" has become the mantra of our world. And this demand for facts has reduced our teaching to a concern for testing, to the near exclusion of the need for synthesis of ideas, toward fresh insight, toward new portraits of reality. The Bible is among the most imaginative books ever written, but the church has too regularly been heard to ask of it, "Did it happen like that?" and "When did it happen?" and "Where?" Instead, we need to nurture an imagination that asks different questions: "How can I picture this scene?" "What does a golden calf look like, and why would the teller of the story use a calf as the would-be god anyway?"

Let's use Exodus 32 again to explore how an enlarging imagination might bring the story to vivid life. We remember that Moses has deputized Aaron to handle any disputes while he and God are chatting on the sacred mountain (Exod. 24:14). Moses quickly disappears on his way up the mountain, and immediately the people "mob" (one possible reading of the word used in 32:1) Aaron and demand that he make "gods" (the Hebrew is the plural noun 'elohim) for them, because Moses has obviously left them in the lurch. Amazingly, Aaron does just that by demanding gold (that gift from the Egyptians!) from them and fashioning it carefully and with skill into a "molten calf." Can you picture it? Ah, how cute—a sweet little calf, gleaming in the firelight! But what do you know about images of bulls in the ancient world? Every ancient culture used the image of a bull as a sign of vast power and strength; the Egyptians and the Babylonians had bull gods in their pantheons. So why have Aaron make a calf god? Could it be that the storyteller is having fun at the expense of other religious ideas? Could the storyteller be saying that calves are cute but not gods at all, or if any sort of god, one not capable of doing much of anything? Could he be saying that these Israelites have seriously lost their minds if they think that a golden calf "brought them out of the land of Egypt" (the exact words of 32:4) instead of YHWH, their God, who precisely "brought them out of the land of Egypt" as the first commandment so clearly said (Exod. 20: 2)? Frederick Buechner has a great line about this scene that I will paraphrase (you may now use it in your sermon, with proper oral attribution, of course): The Israelites at the base of the mountain know what we all have always known, namely, that a god in the hand is worth two in the bush. Now that's imagination!

Part of our problem is that we do not give ourselves enough time to allow our imaginations to work. "Saturday night specials," that is, sermons written on the day before they are preached, do not afford enough time to allow our imaginations to be activated. So read your text well before you intend to preach on it, and don't forget to turn on your imagination. That organ is in there, waiting to bring your text alive, and, like Ezekiel's dry bones, anxious to stand on its feet, a vast and wondrous company of images, ready to invigorate the sermon.

Questions for Reflection

1. Have I implied that the Bible is merely a book of answers to certain modern questions? Have I simply quoted passages from the Bible to prove a desired point without attention to their context?
2. Does my sermon give the impression that a sermon is biblical simply because it includes many biblical quotations?
3. Do I habitually base my sermons on my favorite passages and avoid others I know little about or that may prove difficult?
4. Have I preached the God to whom the Bible points, rather than the Bible itself?
5. Do I inculcate in my sermons the language of the Bible, whose language is in danger of disappearing and/or being seriously misused?
6. Do I use Bible stories as evidence of the Gospel rather than merely stories for their own sake?
7. Do I seek ways to nurture my imagination in order to energize my sermons with vividness and freshness?

Chapter 3

What Not to Say (and What to Say)
at the Beginning

The beginning is the half of the whole.

Hesiod

Well begun is half-done.

English proverb

It is only the first step that costs.
*Madame du Deffand, on the distance that St. Denis, a third-century
martyr, is reputed to have walked carrying his own head*

*He who deliberates fully before taking a step will spend his entire life
on one leg.*

Chinese proverb

Locusts are the Rambos of the insect world.

John Holbert

*I*f these brief aphorisms about beginning are to be believed, once you have
begun a sermon, you are already halfway to the end and will be firmly bal-
anced on both of your legs. However, you may be holding your head in your
hands, a fact that will not only be distinctly uncomfortable but will also make
the ending of the sermon rather difficult. Concerning that locust statement, I
will have more to say later.

Welcome to the world of sermon beginnings. Oodles of ink and megabytes
of musings have been devoted to the subject of how to begin a sermon. As in
the other chapters of this book, we want to show you what not to do as you
begin and to make some suggestions concerning what you might do to start.

An early warning: Avoid like the plague, like a devastating case of Avian
flu, the purchase, theft, or borrowing of any book that promises anything like

35

"1,000 snappy sermon starters." These egregious monstrosities may indeed contain a thousand of something, one or two of which may be snappy (or sappy or crappy or yappy—well, you get the picture). But they will not be real to you; by definition, they will not have arisen from your life, your thought, your heart, your imagination. They will be canned, and like all canned things they will go bad, make you sick, bulge from the top, rot from within, and generally make everyone miserable. However you choose to begin, make that beginning your own. This, of course, goes for the whole sermon, a demand one would think hardly needs voicing, though in a world where pulpit theft appears rampant, from stories that did not happen to you made out to be your personally powerful experience, to the outright pillaging of entire sermons, such a warning, I fear, is very much needed. One might imagine that preachers, at the very least, could obey the Eighth Commandment, and the other nine to boot, I hope, but stories abound of grand larceny perpetrated by some very big-time preachers. Isaiah 6 springs to mind: "Woe is me, for I am lost. I am a person of unclean lips living among other people of unclean lips, because I have caught a glimpse, just a tiny glimmer, of the Lord of Hosts" (au. trans.). Would that that were tattooed on our foreheads!

But I digress, something you should never do in a sermon, but something that may be partially acceptable in a book, since you do not have to read a digression, but you cannot ignore one in a sermon since you are doing your best to listen, and most preachers do not set out orange cones announcing "diverted traffic" before they head off toward uncharted, unannounced, and thoroughly unrelated waters.

To begin is to set oneself effectively to do something, to be at the point of first contact with, to enter upon, to take the first step, to commence, to start. Or in more abstract language, to begin is to broach, to rouse oneself to, to seize hold of, to take in hand, to set oneself to. (All this is from the *Oxford English Dictionary.*) Note the action language in all these definitions: Seizing and taking and broaching sound downright violent. One could think that to begin is to tear into the fabric of the attention of the hearer, to seize her by the ears, twist her head toward your mouth, and bellow the Gospel at a sufficient decibel level so as to ward off those unwelcome intruders—boredom leading to inattention, leading to quiet slumber.

Despite the violent language, sermon beginnings are primarily not designed to gain attention, however much writers on preaching have assumed such a thing. Such a belief makes out congregants to be recalcitrant, unwilling, and incapable listeners who would rather read the newspaper than attend to the sermon, would rather count the number of hymns in a hymnal they happen to know than listen to you, would rather be anywhere than in a pew, fixed in such a way as to have clear sight of the preacher. If that were the case, they would not have come to church now, would they? No, the beginnings of sermons ought not be designed to gain attention. There is not a hungering soul in the church who, upon reading the bulletin (or examining the screen) and finding there either the title of a sermon or at least the announcement that one is about to occur, who does not turn as much attention as he can muster on the one in front of him who is about to speak. The beginning of a sermon does not need to awaken or shock or astound or titillate or even amuse. But it does need to do something.

I find Thomas Long's definition hard to improve upon: "A sermon introduction should make, implicitly or explicitly, a promise to the hearers" (Long 2005, 177). He goes on to say that this promise should have such value that the hearer wants it kept, that it should communicate at the same level (e.g., thoughtful, precise, or emotionally profound) as the rest of the sermon, and that it should anticipate the whole sermon. This definition is what makes my first sentence "Locusts are the Rambos of the insect world" so poor.

What Not to Say at the Beginning

Do Not Overcute Yourself at the Start

I have just added another word to the one-million-word English language, but it is precisely descriptive of why my first sentence was not a promise of anything to come. My text was Joel and his use of a plague of locusts to demonstrate the divine will toward Israel. It is quite true that locusts are nothing else than grasshoppers gone bad (I might now say "on steroids" to stay current) and that scientists still do not know just why on occasion small swarms of chomping grasshoppers can suddenly become great clouds of marauding locusts, eating their way through vast fields of grain, leaving stripped devastation behind.

In my attempt to be cute and clever, I came up with that Rambo line. Though I think it important to use contemporary cultural references in sermons, the Rambo reference is now dated, the world having moved on to other things in a vain quest for ultimate meaning in the new and the now. As I remember it, and it has been more than twenty years since this sermon was preached, the point was certainly not a lecture on the finer points of etymological lore about our friends the grasshoppers. I must assume that I was really after a view of God and was using Joel to get me there. There was no promise in the first line beyond a promise that this preacher was after the clever rather than the theologically serious. No one hearing that first sentence could have had the faintest notion what this day's sermon was going to be about. In short, do as I say, not what I did!

Do Not Tell a Joke to Start Your Sermon

By "joke" I mean a story of a fairly brief sort of the "man goes into a bar" variety. Jokes disembodied from the sermon, jokes used to draw a laugh, to loosen up the crowd before the main event of the sermon, jokes told to suggest to the congregation that the preacher is just one funny guy or gal should suffer the fate of any sermonic element that does not add to the unified whole of the sermon. In short, chuck it! Chain it to the bottomless pit that burns with unquenchable fire. Or a la Dante, put it in the mouth of Satan in hell, head-down in ice at the lowest level. Sermons are no place for jokes. Preachers should banish from their beginnings lines like "Have you heard the one about . . ." or "A priest and a nun and a rabbi . . ."

Humor, of course, is another matter. Humor can be our friend, breaking down barriers of bigotry and fear—but humor that arises out of our words and situations and contexts. Sermonic humor is never used to ridicule or mock; satire and cruel irony rarely work in preaching, whether employed at the beginning or middle or end. Church life has almost an infinite series of opportunities to ridicule, make fun of, pillory, assault, and attack any number of people and situations. Preachers must resist such easy targets with all their might. Liberals beware! Fundamentalists are Christians too. Fundamentalists on alert! Liberals are Christians too, no matter how hard it is for you to imagine it. Let your humor be gentle, genuine, real, part of the fabric of your experience.

Do Not Tell a Long Emotional Story at the Start

Preachers are privy to all sorts of stories, events, and experiences laden with deeply emotional freight and are tempted regularly to share these gems with the congregation. Such things may surely be done, with proper authorization from the people involved, of course, but rarely does it work at a sermon's beginning. This is so for multiple reasons.

First, once I have been doused in a bath of warm romantic suds, I long for slumber, not further serious talk. If you try strangely to warm my heart as you start with a story about a marvelous hospital visit where God was very real, I am eager to feel, not to think. It is wonderful to help me feel, but you ought to save that for later if you want me to attend to whatever else you want me to hear. Fred Craddock's great line is surely true: "The longest journey anyone ever takes is from the head to the heart." But if you begin in the heart and attempt to move me deeply at the start, the return ticket likely will not be punched.

Second, if you begin with something heart-rending, achingly painful, I will likely get so stuck in the pain that I will not be able to escape to listen to anything else. Stories of deep emotion (the preacher's divorce, the sudden death of one of the church's pillars, a community tragedy) have a way of overpowering all else and should be used very sparingly and, I would suggest, never at the beginning of a sermon.

Third, it could be argued, and I might be one to join the fray, that emotional stories in sermons have the primary purpose of moving the hearers. On the face of it, that is not necessarily an evil thing. Rhetorical studies tell us that speeches designed to persuade are complex mixtures of content, person, and emotion, all employed to energize, to disturb, to challenge, and to support, among many other goals. Manipulation may also occur. Too often the emotional stories I have heard in sermons seemed especially designed to manipulate emotions, to draw from me a sob, to "not leave a dry eye in the house." And there is little doubt that preachers have ready access to deeply emotional encounters that only a stone would not respond to. But, let's be honest. Why do we preachers employ such stories? Is it to illustrate the wondrous power of the divine in lives too often characterized by the mundane round of days, the human equivalent of a Tahitian sunset, a flower-bedecked hillside, a moonlight shaft over a quiet lake? Or is it done for the effect it has on the hearers, the sob, the tear, a throat's catch? Every preacher should ask this question with as much probity as she can muster.

If such stories find their way into your sermons, do not begin with them. And if they do find their way into your sermons, ask yourself why. Please.

Do Not Blither In to the Sermon

I have always loved the word *blither* and its many delightful synonyms: *blather, piffle, prattle,* among other equally luscious words. They cast an onomatopoeic spell whenever they show up, and they wonderfully describe too many of the sermon beginnings I have heard—and done. Essentially, all these marvelous words mean, "to speak trivially." When I blither at the beginning of a sermon, I do the very worst thing I can do; I announce that what I have to say today is unfortunately trivial. And just why anyone would care to listen to such twaddle (there is another synonym) is beyond me.

When I blither at the beginning of a sermon, I do any one or more of several egregious things. I may exhaust the hearer with excessive detail in the manner of a long-winded friend who just cannot tell a story without copious bits of information that add nothing: "My wife and I went to a restaurant last night; you perhaps know it—uh, Mariano's? No, that wasn't it. El Pinto? I don't think so. La Cucaracha? I'm not sure. Honey, do you remember the name of that restaurant we went to last night?" The point of telling this story has absolutely nothing to do with the name of the restaurant. Preachers sometimes blither like that with an unnecessary snowstorm of information. Or blithering may simply offer obscure pieces of information that obfuscate the start, rather like the great clouds of steam sent up by a giant rocket. We have not assembled to witness the steam, but to see the rocket launched. To blither is to trivialize a subject at the very start. When I blither to begin a sermon, I do not use an emotionally charged story, nor do I tell a putrid joke, nor do I "overcute" myself. What I do is trivialize, obscure, or waste time in any one of the following ways (please feel free to add your own examples which, like the Markan demoniac's demons, are legion):

- I announce something that happened to me on the way to church that morning, proclaiming to the congregation that this thought occurred to me not thirty minutes ago. My listeners can almost bet that what I experienced at that recent moment has little or nothing to do with the sermon they sincerely hope I have been working on for some time longer than the previous half an hour. This is blithering at its loathsome best.
- My opening sentence begins with a very long circumstantial clause, carefully and completely disguising what the main verb of this sentence may be, something like the following: "As I was coming to church this morning, imagining all your wonderful faces arrayed before me, remembering the beauty of the sanctuary during last night's wedding of Bill and Joan, how happy they were, how proud their parents were, how well Jennifer played and sang . . ." By now, three-quarters of the congregation have given up entirely and have decided that next week they will stay in bed.
- I begin with the good idea of using a recent movie to set the subject of my sermon. But I take too long getting to it. It may sound like this: "Last night my husband and I went to a movie. We went to that theater, you know, that specializes in foreign films. We like foreign films; they seem so much more serious than what Hollywood puts out these days. And we do not at all mind reading the subtitles, because we are fast readers. Besides, the people who go to these sorts of films are always more interesting than those who go to the blockbusters, don't you think? Anyway, we saw this movie, and my, it was so good. You would love it; we recommend it highly." Are you still with me? I didn't think so.

- I begin with something so obscure that I have to spend a great deal of time explaining it and why I am using it at all: "I was watching television one night last week, very late. Had a hard time sleeping. It was about midnight, I think. Anyway, I was racing through the channels. You know how you do, surfing around. I stopped at channel 483. Do you get that one? It was a show about a sixteenth-century gun maker, can't remember his name—Gruber maybe, German, I guess. In any case, it described how this guy had accidentally made gunpowder out of baking soda and ashes, I think it was, or maybe coal; I'm not sure. It just goes to show how funny things can happen." Well, it shows something, but "funny" may have little to do with it. And why am I telling this anyway?
- I begin by reading parts of "The Love Song of J. Alfred Prufrock," by T. S. Eliot. It is without doubt a very suggestive poem, rich in meaning. I loved it in college and have read it once or twice since. It is immensely sad, filled with images that conjure hopelessness, mundane living, and the pain of aging. My plan is to contrast it with the joy of the Gospel. It is, unfortunately, 132 lines long and not immediately understandable by those who have never read it or who have read very little other serious poetry, so I try to cut it to the pithy bits. Maybe I include the first five lines, plus that line about "daring to eat a peach," and "I grow old, I grow old, I shall wear the bottoms of my trousers rolled," concluding with "That is not what I meant at all, That is not it, at all." There is little doubt that after that, the congregation will be hungry for the Gospel for sure! But this is still blithering, albeit very high-class blithering.

A Sermon Beginning Should Match the Whole Sermon in Its Choice of Communicational Type

This is a bit more of a subtle concern than the previous four things you ought not do as you begin to preach. But I think it is very important to announce the promise of your beginning not just with your choice of words but also with the way in which you express them. I agree with David Buttrick: "After an introduction, people should be ready to hear a sermon, and to hear it in a certain way" (Buttrick 1987, 90). It could be said that the four problems of sermon beginnings I have just discussed may be summarized in this fifth concern. Being overcute, telling jokes, leading with long emotional stories, and blithering are each examples of beginnings that do not match the remainder of the sermon. In each case, I do one thing in a certain emotional tone, but I do not continue that tone in the remainder of the sermon. Let us review each in turn and show the dangers of tonal disparity between beginnings and what happens in the rest of the sermon.

My own example of *an overcute beginning* set up a tone for the sermon that the rest of the sermon did not emulate. The opening sentence, "Locusts are the Rambos of the insect world," promised some sort of discussion about insects, crucial information that the listeners would need to have if they were to understand the purpose of the sermon. No such information was needed, however. The sermon was not about locusts and their odd relationships to grasshoppers, but about the presence and power of God in the lives and destinies of nations, past and present. Not only is the content of the beginning not helpful, but the aphoristic cuteness is hardly sustained for long—in fact, not past the first line! The "cute" beginning did not match the sermon's overall tone at all—a bad beginning indeed!

By its very nature, *a joke* as a beginning cannot match the tone of the rest, unless the rest of the sermon is a series of jokes. If that is true, the preacher needs to resign his pulpit immediately and proceed to the nearest comedy club in search of honest work. I assume that preachers begin with a joke because they are trying to "get people on their side" and indicate that they are funny folks. In addition, they are looking to warm up the crowd. The club circuit wants you! (But be warned: I hear the world of stand-up is a tough place, where only the fittest and the filthiest survive.) Jokes do not belong at the beginning of a sermon, period.

I hate to imagine a sermon where *a long emotional story* at the beginning is matched by a long, equally emotional sermon! The image of sobbing congregants, holding on to one another for dear life as they stagger up the tear-soaked aisles, the preacher having ripped out their hearts and guts with twenty minutes of fervent manipulation, is a picture that I wish to push far from my mind. Unless that little shop of horrors is made real, a reality devoutly not to be wished, a deeply emotional beginning will necessarily not match the rest of the sermon. And, it should be noted, very few will remember anything of the rest in any case if the opening gambit is so emotional as to wipe the rest away.

I sincerely hope that a blithering opening will not be matched by a blithering middle and end. If I blither at the beginning, I in effect warn my listeners that they can expect further trivial blithering from me, if they choose to continue to listen, which most of them, I imagine, will not.

What to Say at the Beginning

Now that I have warned you about several dangerous minefields that await the unwary preacher as she dreams up ways to start a sermon, I wish to spend some time talking about ways sermons might be begun effectively. There is probably no end to the positive possibilities, but because you do not plan to spend the remainder of your life reading about starting a sermon, rather than actually starting one, I will limit my suggestions to a few categories only.

I also wish to use the same biblical text to exemplify the various ways one can begin. That text is Exodus 32, the so-called golden calf story, though a more careful reading will suggest issues that move well beyond gold and calves. Any preacher knows that the focus of a sermon can shift around under the influence of the actual creation of the sermon, but for our purposes, let us say that the focus of this sermon will be leadership.

Tips for Using Stories at the Beginning

There is a vast literature on the use of stories in preaching, but the choice of what sorts of stories may be used comes down to two words: appropriate and engaging.

The choice of the opening story must be appropriate in the light of the disasters enumerated in the first section of this chapter, and the story must be engaging in order to keep the attention of the hearers, who while readily offering their attention as the preacher begins, will just as readily withdraw that attention if given any opportunity to do so. This does not mean that your hearers are venal or lazy or cruel; it simply means they are human and need help to stay in the boat with you. As you put your oar into the sermonic waters, you should hand them an oar to join you in the pull. Or to shift the metaphor, hearers need a consistent tug at the earlobe in order to follow the flow of a sermon. I will say much more about these tugs in the chapter about what ought not be said in the middle of a sermon, but I need to address it here, because hearers can be lost rather quickly if the beginning goes awry.

"Moses dripped sweat as he stumbled down the mountain. Conversations with God can be exhausting." With this opening I promise my hearers that they are about to hear a story, a retelling of the story of Exodus 32, which they have probably just heard read to them. I have begun in the middle of the story and have focused on Moses. Because the focus of the sermon is leadership, I have announced to my hearers that somehow Moses is going to have something to do with that topic (Let's say my title is "Will the Real Leader Please Stand Up?"). From this opening, they do not yet know whether the entire sermon will be a retold Bible story (it will be, in this case) or whether I am just going to begin with a retelling and then move on to some kind of explanation. Remember that my beginning should promise both content and tone. Hence, if my beginning tone is the pleasure of a story and if I plan to move away from story toward explanation later in the sermon, I run the risk of losing the story pleasure in sermonic explanation. I cannot overestimate this danger. How many sermons have we heard or preached that lead with a gripping story, calling on every ear in the church to attend with eagerness, only to be dropped into a dry hole of explanation, a talking about the story to make a series of theological and/or practical points about the story, bringing near universal disappointment to those same ears who turn away sadly to attend to other sounds: the explosion of the air-conditioning compressor, the whimpering of the grandchild, the gentle snore of Uncle Fred, the tap-tap of patent leather on the tiled floor.

Unlike the first beginning, I might start in the modern world to get at my concern for real leadership. I might choose any number of examples from the ranks of leaders who are admired and well-known (e.g., Martin Luther King Jr., Franklin Roosevelt, Mahatma Gandhi) or persons less well-known publicly but who have played important leadership roles for the preacher (e.g., a favorite teacher, a well-loved minister, a parent, a parishioner). I could say, "Our world has regularly offered examples of real leadership," and proceed to offer famous and not-so-famous examples.

As always in the use of stories, care needs to be taken that the story actually illustrates the sermon topic of the day. Stories, if they are especially good, have a way of escaping their bounds and taking on a life of their own. The preacher must always seek to control the chosen story, to bid it make plain the theme of this sermon. Many a sermon has begun with an excellent story, only to introduce into the hearts of the hearers multiple avenues, any one of which can become thoroughfares away from today's chosen theme. Another danger of the opening story is that it is so good, so gripping, so moving, that any material after it appears dull, even if it is the biblical text of the day. Like the powerful Bible story as a beginning, followed by numbing explanation, so a powerful modern story can overwhelm the hearer, leaving her trapped in its spell.

Other Ways to Start the Sermon

Do not start with dull stuff. This advice may appear so obvious as to not need naming, but lengthy exegetical or historical insights (e.g., "How important leadership is in our world! Moses was a great leader, and a smart one too. In the world of ancient Egypt where he was raised, he must have received a fine education from those scribes, perhaps learning about architecture, the risings and settings of the great Nile River, the very life-blood of Egypt . . ."), long-winded sociological reports (e.g., "Scientists tell us that human beings have long had a love affair with bananas. In the arboreal forests of Equatorial Africa, our simian ancestors craved the yellow fruit, a fact proven by the stomach contents of well-preserved monkey mummies. But just how did we become the leaders we are today, evolving as we did from these banana-loving relatives?"), or special interests of the preacher (e.g., "Many of you know just how much I love NASCAR. The speed, the power, the noise, the rich smells of gasoline and oil and burning tires are all like perfume to me. Why, I went to a race just last week, and I was in my element. It was just so, oh, I don't know, just so beautiful! And the leadership of those drivers!"). NASCAR is definitely a popular activity, but, I think it fair to say, it is also an acquired taste, and one that has not yet been acquired by all.

I hope you noted as well that all three of these examples possess the distinct possibility of not revealing just what in the world this sermon may be about: Moses and his possible upbringing, the history of bananas, and a love of NASCAR hardly preview what I may have in mind for my flock today. If you do not choose to start with a story, then open quick and sharp with a straightforward declarative sentence: "Today I want to explore something very important: how can we identify real leadership." Or "Our world has always looked for and prized real leadership." Or "Who do you think are real leaders in our world today?" These simple sentences avoid the problem of dribbling in, and they make a clear promise to the hearer that today's subject is in fact leadership.

Point out immediately the portion of the Scripture lesson that energized the sermon for you. "Though this passage from Exodus is often called "The Golden Calf," what struck me when I read it this time is the lengthy discussion between Moses and Aaron and just how differently Moses and Aaron react to those who made that calf in the first place. It makes me ask why Moses sounds like a leader to me, and why Aaron sounds like something else." The very reason that I came to preach this sermon on this text is this central observation. By sharing it up front, I invite my listeners into my homiletical workshop.

Begin by reading aloud a recent newspaper or magazine report. Have the newspaper or magazine in hand to add credibility, or if your church is so wired, pop up on the screen a news or film clip. Any of these will grab instant attention and interest; however, they may also create the dangers I have mentioned. Read reports have a certain tone that can be unlike the rest of the sermon. Even more, a snappy film clip adds color and sound and movement, playing in to the near universal love of film in our culture. You may certainly gain attention, but the sermon that follows, in the main devoid of the multisensory power of the film, can quickly pale. Do not set yourself up for sermonic disaster by demonstrating just how much less interesting you really are than your media competition! This is not at all to say that filmic clips are to be avoided completely, but they should be used with more care than they sometimes are.

Begin with a congregational memory or hope. Every congregation wants to be reminded of those times in its past when many felt that they really were being the church: a mission trip, a peace rally, a demonstration at city hall, meals served to hurricane evacuees. Nothing binds a group of hearers together more tightly than a shared experience. Even those who are new, who did not participate in the particular events, will swell with pride to hear such stories of the church's past. I was once asked to preach for the 125th anniversary of a congregation's founding. I had never been in the church and knew not a single member. I began with a fictional portrait of the congregation through the years, pointing to now empty pews and naming those who had gone before (making up names as I went!), recounting events that occur in every church's life: baptisms, weddings, and conflicts about the neighborhood, about pastoral styles, about war. I was amazed when many members of the now much-smaller congregation said things like, "I did not know you knew Mary" and "I was surprised to be reminded of that time of conflict" and "We did have trouble with pastor Ted for a time, but we grew to love him." Memory is a great glue that can bind and seal a community of faith.

But, of course, memory is not enough. The God we worship is always in the business of the new, so memories are not named for purposes of nostalgia, but to renew hope for the future. In my sermon I was careful to say that the congregation's life had not ended in "the good old days" (which are inevitably more old than good) but that a bright future still lies ahead for the souls who dared to embrace it.

So now you may begin. Ladies and gentlemen, start your sermons!

Questions for Reflection

1. Are my openings just cute, or do they introduce the Good News? Have I been too cute at the beginning of my sermons?
2. Do I habitually tell unrelated jokes as I begin my sermons?
3. Do I begin with long emotional stories?
4. Have I blithered my way into the sermon, rather than started sharply?
5. Does my sermon begin in the same tone as the rest of the sermon?

6. Do I vary my openings, sometimes beginning with the Bible's story and sometimes with an appropriate modern story, current event, or shared congregational memory?
7. Is the first sentence of my sermon sharp and short?
8. Have I made clear to my hearers at the beginning exactly what moved me to the subject I have chosen, just how I got to the idea for today's sermon?

Chapter 4

What Not to Say (and What to Say) about Your People

Pastor: "I know just how you feel."
Parishioner: "No, you don't."

Preacher, to her nine-year-old daughter: "How can I be a better preacher?"
Daughter: "Don't use so many words kids like me don't understand."

*Y*ou may wonder why this chapter is necessary. We already know what to say about our people from the pulpit—good things, things that challenge them while encouraging and empowering them. Onto the next chapter. Not so fast. This chapter is about subliminal messages—what we imply about our people by the things we say. Every sermon we preach says something about our people, how we think of them in relation to ourselves, their needs, their weaknesses, their abilities, and their blind spots. A vehement conviction that you don't need to read this chapter may be a sign of just how much you do need to read it.

In the table of contents of his book *Pitfalls in Preaching*, Norbert Becker lists a number of preacher-types, each of which embodies a bad habit or pitfall he warns us to avoid. They are, the Essayist, the Entertainer, the Moralizer, the Legalist, the Dogmatist, the Loner, the Professional, the Emotionalist, the Lambaster, the Alien, the Bore, the Rambler, the Repeater, and the Plagiarizer (Becker, *Pitfalls in Preaching*). So many choices, so little time!

As if those weren't enough pitfalls, now I'm going to add four more. These have to do specifically with how we think about and relate to people in our sermons: the Isolationist, the Stereotyper, the Underestimator, and the Compartmentalizer. There is a positive flipside to each, which offers guidance for what to say about our people in our sermons. Isolationism can become identification, denigration (negative stereotyping) can become commendation, underestimation can become respectful education and compartmentalization can become unification.

What Not to Say about Your People

First, we'll attend to any budding negative habits, examining what not to say about our people, and work our way around to some positive advice about what to say.

The Isolationist

A former generation of preachers, influenced by the neo-orthodoxy of Karl Barth, believed that what we would call congregational exegesis is unnecessary. The preacher shouldn't spend his time trying to understand the needs and situation of the congregation in its cultural context. He shouldn't worry about what listeners' daily lives are like, what books they read, what Web sites they visit, what shows they watch, what traumas they're going through at home and at work. God's word makes its own hearing.

I agree with that last statement. I believe that God is the presence and power at the heart of preaching, that revelation does not depend on the eloquence of our word choices or the pertinence of our illustrations to our people. I believe that the Holy Spirit can speak to people even through the most halting, faltering preacher. Still, it can only help our preaching for us to know our audience.

Preaching conveys the Word of God, which I understand as the Self-Communication of God, not verbatim words from God from the preacher's lips. Preaching conveys the presence of God through human words. The major Protestant reformers agreed that there is a sacramental quality to preaching. In sacraments we respond to the Grace God offers. Exegeting the congregation is a way of responding to God's Grace offered in preaching.

Someone once defined preaching as "a risk God takes." It's no sin to minimize the risk, so let's not ignore our listeners' situations: their anxieties, their dreams, their foibles, their faults, their guilt, their glory. If God can speak through a boring, incoherent sermon, it stands to reason that God can also speak through a coherent, compelling sermon.

Preachers throughout history have known that it is as important to exegete the congregation as it is to exegete the text. Jesus certainly did, choosing examples from farm, hearth, and synagogue to speak to his listeners. These included mustard seeds, returning sons, lost coins, and apparently dead fig trees.

A prime example from the early days of Christian preaching is Pope Gregory the Great (540–604) who wrote *The Book of Pastoral Rule* in 591, shortly after his election as bishop of Rome. The Rule deals with the responsibilities of the bishop in preaching and pastoral care. In a section with the heading "Differently to Be Addressed Are," Gregory lists thirty-seven pairs of opposite human conditions, including men and women, rich and poor, the joyful and the sad, and the humble and the haughty (Gregory the Great 1894, 1–3, 8).

The preacher who does not believe in exegeting her congregation is almost inevitably going to become a bore. The concepts she preaches about will lack flesh, blood, and traction in people's daily lives. Since she does not bother to keep up with popular culture, she is unable to connect biblical themes and people with contemporary themes and people. Fred Craddock, Haddon Robinson, and others have suggested that boredom is a form of evil and that it is a sin to bore people with the Bible. They are absolutely right. The central point of Nora Tubbs Tisdale's book on congregational exegesis, *Preaching as Local Theology and Folk Art*, is that a sermon cannot be faithful to a text if the preacher has not made the effort to make it fitting to a congregation. Tisdale calls on John Calvin's notion of accommodation to support her conviction. Calvin speaks of "accommodation" as "being part of God's gracious divine action through which God takes the initiative and rhetorically bridges—through word and deed—the great gulf that exists between human beings and God" (Tisdale 1997, 35–36). To refuse to exegete our congregations is to disdain God's own rhetorical approach!

A habit of the Isolationist is the use of jargon. Norbert Becker refers to the preacher who uses specialized words and language of biblical scholars and theologians as "the Alien." This preacher sets himself above and at a distance from the people by his use of jargon. He tosses around terms like *apocalyptic, atonement, eschatology, justification,* and *sola scriptura* to show that he knows something his people don't, a habit that springs either from insecurity or arrogance. Either way, it is an ineffective way of communicating with an audience.

A preacher I know asked her nine-year-old daughter "How can I preach better?" Her daughter replied, "Don't use words kids like me can't understand. One is OK now and then, but when you put a whole lot of them together, I stop listening."

Immersed in our specialized "in-house" language, we can be oblivious to the fact that words whose meanings we assume people know actually sound like jargon to some. Examples are *sin, righteous, salvation, Gospel, kingdom of God, died for our sins,* and *eucharistic.* Victor Paul Furnish, emeritus professor of New Testament at Perkins School of Theology, tells of a weekend lecture series he presented at a local church. After the final lecture, a man came up to him holding his Bible. "Dr. Furnish, I've really enjoyed your talks. But I've searched my whole Bible and haven't been able to find the 'extra Jesus' you've talked about."

Can we give people back their theological vocabulary with brief explanations without overdefining and qualifying everything we say? I think we can. I think we have no choice if we want to communicate the Good News. Accomplished preacher and compassionate pastor The Rev. Dr. Zan Holmes, who taught homiletics for many years at Perkins School of Theology, used to tell his students, "Do your homework, but don't preach your homework. Use your homework to preach the Gospel."

The Isolationist is first in my picture gallery of "What Not to Say about Your People" because from this unwillingness to exegete one's congregation come all the other negative preacherly habits. When you don't know your people, their questions and concerns, you fall back on stereotypes (usually negative), you underestimate them, and you fail to preach to the total person—mind, heart, and will—because you do not know the total person.

The Stereotyper

Do not engage in negative stereotyping, shaping your sermons around negative judgments about your people's identity. Exegeting the listeners of your congregation, exploring their strengths and weaknesses, is not the same as negatively stereotyping them. In my experience, negative stereotypes are limiting, and they signal that the speaker would rather call it a day than proclaim a new day through the Good News of Jesus Christ. The stereotyping can be blatant, a set piece of mental furniture the pastor sits in whenever she prepares her sermons, the set way she applies every text to her context. Here are some examples of negative stereotypes I've heard pastors utter over the years:

> My congregation is a cross section of George Bush's Texas. There is a lot I can't say.
> The people in my congregation are old and tired. They don't want to do anything in the community.
> My parishioners would rather write checks than get their hands dirty.
> My congregation chews up its pastors and spits them out every couple of years.

Even if the stereotype has a big grain of truth in it, generalizing it and making it our lens for ministry and preaching only serves to reinforce the negative. That, as we know, is not the purpose of preaching on any given Sunday.

The stereotyping can be more subtle, oozing out in seemingly innocent phrases. I remember hearing a pastor who, whenever he presented a challenging message or call to action, habitually said, "Come on now, Church, I know this is a stretch for you, but listen up." I got really sick of hearing that phrase. At the time I was a graduate student and filling in at pulpits every Sunday I could, since a couple of colleagues were having health problems. I had three small children and was seeking to be a good wife, mother, friend, church member, student, and pastor. Did he know to whom he was talking? Maybe I sound like I took his phrase too personally. But how else is anyone in the congregation to take it? Did he really know to whom he was speaking? Did he think that living by a challenging Gospel was a stretch for the doctor in the third row who spent three months of every year at a clinic in Calcutta doing free medical work? Did he think he needed to chide the woman in the fifth row who had been caring for a chronically ill husband for twenty-two years? Is gracious self-sacrifice a "stretch" for her? I was insulted for them. And, okay, I was insulted for myself as well. But I also repent of every time I've caricatured a whole group on the basis of their politics, economics, education or lack thereof, or anything else. My definition of a caricature is a cartoonish depiction of someone's face that exaggerates the unappealing features for comic effect. Is that really what we want to do in our sermons?

Stereotyping that oozes through in our sermon illustrations

Jonathan Mellette, a pastor participating in a Doctor of Ministry course I taught recently, preached a sermon in class on John 2:1–11, the story of Jesus changing water into wine at the wedding in Cana. Rev. Mellette said, "Mary comes to Jesus. She says, 'They have no wine.' Now men, we know what that means. We know that when your wife says, 'We're out of milk,' you're going to buy milk. And we know that when your wife says, 'The grass needs to be mowed,' you're going to mow the grass. We don't have to be asked something to know we're being asked something."

As I listened, I thought, "Oh, no. Where's he going with this? Women as nags like Mary?" If he had stopped there, that would have been a prime example of a negative stereotype oozing through a sermon illustration. But he continued: "Women are well aware of this dynamic too. When men say, 'I can't find my keys,' we're really saying, 'Please stop doing everything you're doing and help me!' When we say, 'I'm getting hungry,' we're really saying, 'Since you're not doing anything anyway, could you take a break from paying the bills, put the baby down, quit folding the sheets, and make me a sandwich?'"

So we all, not just women and not just men, make statements of fact that are really pleas for someone to take action. That works. Nobody is negatively stereotyped. We all nod in amused recognition because we see ourselves in this example and we stay on board as the sermon rolls on. (Mellette 2010).

Each of us needs to ask ourselves: Who are the characters in my illustrations, and what roles do they play? Do my stories feature hapless men learning from wise women? Or the reverse? Years ago, I heard a bishop preach a retirement service at an annual conference. The retirees and their spouses were all sitting in the front row. At that time, all the spouses were female. The bishop was preaching on the sending out of the seventy, encouraging the pastors to continue to follow their vocations into retirement wherever that might lead them. In speaking of the obstacles they had faced so far, he said, "You would get the news that you were moving. And you knew it wouldn't be easy breaking the news. Objections awaited you at home: "I've just changed the wallpaper in the powder room, and you're telling me we're moving?" If I had been one of those women sitting there, I would have thought to myself, "A lifetime of standing by a spouse in the ministry and I'm caricatured as being obsessed with my wallpaper?"

I say we leave the insults to the stand-up comedians. If we're going to preach in the name and spirit of the one who taught us to love our neighbors as ourselves, we need to let that light shine on every person in our congregation and on every person who appears in the stories and examples in our sermons.

The Underestimator

Closely related to the Stereotyper is the Underestimator. I think of the Stereotyper as holding negative caricatures of the identity of his or her hearers. The Underestimator then uses this stereotype to determine the kinds of sermon— the content, the form—he will preach.

The first principle is this: *Don't underestimate the mystery and uniqueness of each human being sitting before you.* When we preach, we bank on a degree of common human experience. We all are born and die; in between we bleed, cry, want to be loved, and fear rejection and loss. We hope that the message we hear from a text will have some resonance with others beyond ourselves. But everyone's experience is not the same.

A pastor told me of a recent Sunday worship service in which he included a renewal of marriage vows for couples in the congregation who had been married for fifty years or more. He noticed that one woman, recently widowed, had not attended church that day. He called her to tell her, "We missed you on Sunday." She replied, "Well, I just decided to stay home." "I know how you feel," he assured her. "No, you don't," was her response.

I cannot assume that just because I had a miscarriage twenty-three years ago I know exactly how a thirty-year-old woman in my church feels about hers. The ability to respect the mystery of people's uniqueness, both as a group and as individuals, is a gift from God to a preacher. It's possible to backslide, so it's important to be vigilant against the preacherly habit of assuming we know the inner recesses of someone else's experience. People recognize and appreciate genuine respect when they encounter it. It can come through in phrases: "I'm a guest preacher; I don't presume to know all about you and your sufferings," or "I'm going to speak for myself now, and if you recognize yourself in this, then come on in and join me." You'll come up with better phrases, but signal from time to time that you're not underestimating the differences between you and them and that you recognize and respect their uniqueness.

Don't underestimate people's love of variety. Not everybody loves variety, of course. Some people like the same thing every week. They may be the ones who would most benefit from variety. But at any rate, here the "no stereotyping" principle applies to the forms we choose for our sermons: "Oh, my congregation is all engineers. They will hate story sermons." "My congregation has a lot of artists. They will hate three-point sermons." Aim for a variety of sermon forms, and you may be surprised what appeals to whom. Sometimes engineers like to enter into a story sermon that surprises them at the end. Sometimes high school art teachers savor the precision of a sermon that has three points.

Don't underestimate your people's hunger for scriptural knowledge and theological understanding. I could say something like this: "My congregation is mainly blue collar. I don't think they'll respond well to a sermon on the Trinity." Why not? Is the Trinity only for people with master's degrees? Or do I not have a clear enough grasp of what's at stake in the Trinity to preach a clear and compelling sermon about it? Am I secretly afraid I can't answer the "So what?" question regarding the Trinity, about the difference it makes in their lives and mine?

Suppose a preacher were to say, "I uncover a lot in my exegetical work that people wouldn't really be able to understand." Really? It is true that not every exegetical tidbit we turn up in preparing for our sermons has transformative power and deserves to make it into the sermon. But in a sermon on Psalm 121, don't you think people would be interested in the fact that ancient people viewed the sun as dangerous ("The sun shall not strike you by day," v. 6a) and the night as holding terrors ("nor the moon by night," v. 6b). Don't you think they'd be interested in knowing that "keep" throughout the Old Testament and in, for example, 2 Timothy 1:12 indicates "to guard" and that it refers to God's tender preservation of those who trust in God? Wouldn't you want to share with your people that God watches over them in their pilgrimage through this life and into the next in an even more profound way than by the guarantee of physical safety? This information contains what I call "sacred sparks" that can fan faith from ember to flame—but only if we preachers relate these biblical images and concepts to our listeners' fears and to God's faithfulness at the depth of their lives. Out of our own exegetical work with a text, we glean categories, concepts, and images for our own walk with God. Why wouldn't we share them with our congregation? I believe people are hungrier for biblical knowledge and theological understanding than they have been in decades. As I teach and preach in classrooms and churches, I see this desire in people's faces and hear it in their questions. Such a wholesome hunger deserves to be fed, not underestimated.

Don't underestimate people's hunger for the truth. We all hunger for other things besides the truth, of course. We hunger for recognition, and comfort, and wealth, and sexual gratification, and the fountain of youth, and on and on. But don't assume that what we think people want to hear is what, in the long run, they really want and need to hear. We are not called to offer surface messages that sugarcoat life's bitter realities and soften the hard edges of the Gospel's call to sacrifice.

In their book *Make the Word Come Alive: Lessons from the Laity*, Mary Alice Mulligan and Ronald J. Allen interviewed 263 laypeople from twenty-eight congregations. Nine congregations were composed largely of African Americans, sixteen primarily had persons of non-Hispanic European origin, and three were ethnically mixed. The comments from these laypeople were telling. Said one respondent, "If you can't bring issues up, then the church is not doing what it is supposed to do." Another said, "The ministers try to make everything pretty G-rated." Yet another added, "But life isn't like that." Numerous laypeople expressed the desire for preachers to go ahead and "step on their toes" if it will help them mature in the faith (Mulligan and Allen 2005, 74, 96).

The Compartmentalizer

Don't compartmentalize your listeners, speaking to only one aspect of each person's total personhood: head, heart, or will. Classical rhetoric, the art of persuasion, describes three streams of persuasion in a public address: logos (rational ability), ethos (character of the speaker), and pathos (emotional appeal aimed at changing listeners' minds and motivating them to action). An effective speech draws on all three streams of persuasion.

The effective preacher addresses head, heart, and will in every sermon. When preachers compartmentalize their people, they preach one of three kinds of sermons: the hovercraft sermon (directed only to the head), the emotional rollercoaster sermon (the sermon directed only to the heart), or the bootstraps sermon (directed only to the will).

The Hovercraft Sermon

This is the sermon that stays in the head, that deals with concepts that are never illustrated or enfleshed in daily life. They hover over life without landing in any real-life situations. Sermons these days need to teach biblical and theological themes to often biblically illiterate listeners. But they need to do so using images, story, and metaphor. They need to embody their ideas, not just state them. The hovercraft sermon is my name for sermons that hover above real life in a realm of abstractions. Such a sermon stays in the realm of abstract statements about God and the life of faith. The preacher who speaks only to the intellect assumes that if listeners can repeat his ideas, they have experienced the faith. The great preacher Philipps Brooks, speaking in the early twentieth century, commented that many preachers of his day were giving lectures about medicine to sick people, rather than medicine itself (Brooks 1969, 126).

The hovercraft sermon is boring. In the fifth century, Augustine complained that the pagan rhetoricians were spellbinding speakers, while the Christian preachers were dull and lackluster. He sought to borrow principles of interesting, effective public speech and baptize them for Christian preaching. With this in mind, one year I offered a workshop at our Perkins Ministers' Week entitled, "You Can't Bore the Hell Out of People." When it was published in the flyer and on the Web site, it resulted in one letter of complaint from a retired pastor from Oklahoma. He addressed it to me and copied the dean. He said that the use of profanity in a title for a workshop at Perkins School of Theology was a sign of the moral corruption among the younger clergy. (I was very excited that he considered me "young"!) The other result of the title was that 150 people showed up for the workshop.

The hovercraft sermon is boring because it stays in the realm of concepts. While the concepts may be important and even phrased in memorable ways, there are no examples, no anecdotes, no images, no stories we can relate to our own lives.

The Emotional Roller Coaster Sermon

I like roller coasters—sort of. They make me feel something, that's for sure. I'm never bored when I'm on one. I may feel a little dizzy, but never bored.

Sometimes in the middle of a rollercoaster ride, the thought comes to me, "Why am I subjecting myself to this?" But then the next dip comes and I'm distracted from this larger question.

The danger of an emotionally manipulative sermon is that it is an emotional appeal that does not bother to consult with the mind and will. When we stir up people's emotions without tying them to a biblical and theological message, what are they to do with their stirred-up emotions? People are moved by lots of things that aren't the Gospel. Stirring emotions in and of itself is not preaching the Gospel. The trouble with sermons that are strong on pathos to the neglect of ethos and logos is that the preacher may be manipulating the emotions of listeners to ends that do not match the Gospel: "If you believe, you'll be blessed." "If you believe, you'll send more money to my ministry." "If you don't believe as we say you should, hell awaits you."

The Bootstraps Sermon

The old expression is that "you need to pull yourself up by your bootstraps." A sermon directed toward the will that doesn't go through the logic and the emotions is a moralizing sermon. Moralizing is when we point people toward what they ought to be doing or ought not to be doing without pointing them toward the resources of Grace, of God at work within them that makes that activity or refraining from that activity possible. It reminds me of the seminar I went to several years ago at the Philadelphia Convention Center. It was in the early 1990s. It was called "Your Best You in '92." The day featured a series of motivational speeches. I remember a peppy one by Olympic gymnast Mary Lou Retton and a gruffer one by General Norman Schwarzkopf of Desert Storm fame.

The final talk of the day was by a young man I'd never heard of. He made his way to the podium, his posture not conveying the confidence I would have expected of a motivational speaker. Once there, he looked down for longer than was comfortable for us the audience. Then he began to speak: "I've been making motivational talks for years. And I realized today that I just can't do it anymore." Now he had our attention! "Trying to grow in life by giving yourself pep talks is like turning up the thermostat and turning up the thermostat, and then, at the end of the day, realizing that there is no furnace connected to your thermostat. We only grow in wisdom and maturity as we turn to God. God is the furnace."

I believe what the young man was saying is that he had experienced a conversion. He had spent years making self-help speeches, telling people what to do by the strength of their own will. He had come to realize that he had been moralizing. He now saw that they could not do what he had been nudging them to do without God's Grace forgiving and empowering them to action.

The cumulative effect of the bootstraps approach is to undermine people's self-confidence and to enhance their guilt. They don't have to come to church for that. They can get that anywhere. Let's do something different.

Whenever we challenge people to change their behavior or attitudes, we need to connect that change to the power that alone can make it happen: the presence and power of the God of Jesus Christ working in our innermost lives by the agency of the Holy Spirit.

What to Say about Your People

Isolationism Becomes Identification

Isolationism needs to give way to the dynamic of identification. Identification is a central dynamic of communication described by the Greek and Roman teachers of persuasive speech (rhetoric). It was important that the listeners identify with the speaker and recognize common interests, experiences, and motivations. Teacher of preaching Craig Loscalzo points out that identification doesn't mean placating people or always following their lead in our preaching. It doesn't mean adopting a condescending relationship with them in which we assume we know their needs. It comes from authentic relationship with them, an ongoing conversation between the daily lives we and they live and the faith we profess together (Loscalzo 1992, 20). Twentieth-century philosopher Kenneth Burke suggested that people are persuaded when we talk their talk through "speech, gesture, tonality, order, image, attitude, and idea, identifying your ways with theirs" (Burke 1969, 55). Identification works by the dynamic of "empathetic imagination." Fred Craddock defines empathetic imagination as "the capacity to achieve a large measure of understanding of another person without having had the person's experiences" (Craddock 1985, 95)

Identification means discerning the questions the congregation is asking and addressing them in one's sermons. Burke believes that "critical and imaginative works are answers to questions posed by the situation in which they arose" (Burke 1973, 1). Any public communication, whether novel, speech, or work of art, is an attempt by its creator to answer certain questions being asked by his or her context. Our task as preachers, then, is to identify with our people by searching out the questions they are asking and responding to them in our sermons.

Many preachers have the experience of running their sermons by a close friend or family member to receive candid feedback. When I did that in my earlier preaching days, a particular loved one would sometimes say things like, "Why are you telling me this?" or "Why should I care about this?" Those questions were hard to hear, but helpful.

In his book *The Roundtable Pulpit: Where Leadership and Preaching Meet*, John McClure recommends what he calls a "collaborative homiletic," in which consultation with the congregation is built in to the process of sermon preparation. The result is an emergent word, an "interactive persuasion," and a sermon in which the preacher is host rather than answer-giver (McClure 1995). Wesley Allen calls this dynamic a "conversational homiletic" (Allen 2005, 10).

Identification means preaching to the whole person—mind, emotions, and will. In order to do that, of course, we need genuinely to care about the people we preach to. In his book *Speaking the Truth in Love: Christian Public Rhetoric*, Daniel R. Berger says, "Love is necessary for spiritual speaking" and "Love is the foundation, the motivation for the message and the attitude of delivery in Christian Rhetoric" (Berger 2007, 68, 71). In writing about the role of rhetoric in teaching and preaching, theologian John Sullivan looks to Paul's insight in 1 Corinthians 13: "If I speak in the tongues of mortals and of angels, but do not have love, I am a noisy gong or a clanging cymbal." Says Sullivan, "Speaking with love matches the principle I have encountered as ineluctably at work, even if it is never explicitly articulated: 'we don't care what you know unless and until we know that you care'" (Sullivan 2009).

Stereotyping (Denigration) Becomes Commendation

Earlier, I mentioned several negative stereotypes I've heard from preachers about their congregations. This isn't the whole story, though, because over the years I've also heard many commendations:

> My congregation has a real heart for missions.
> My congregation is committed to the community around it.
> My congregation is beginning to realize that its best years are not behind it.
> My congregation really came through for me and my family when we went through our tough times.

In his book *They Like to Never Quit Praisin' God*, Frank Thomas recommends that preachers identify their congregation's negative "core beliefs," those assumptions about their identity and worth that are contrary to the Gospel. These core beliefs can show up both in individual and group attitudes.

Examples might be "Our best years are behind us," "I've made too many mistakes for God to forgive me now," "I am worthless," or "Our wealth will cushion us from life's sufferings."

No matter what, if it's negative, hopeless, or selfish, it's a core belief that is contrary to the Good News of God through Jesus Christ. Thomas recommends that, guided by the text, we expose our people's negative core belief, overturn it with the truth of the Gospel, then celebrate the change that reversal makes in our lives alone and together.

Bringing the power of the Good News to bear on the negative core beliefs of our congregation is not the same as negative stereotyping.

In my Introduction to Preaching classes I talk about the strategy of "commendation." This is not just giving people a spoonful of sugar to make the medicine seem less bitter. For example: I got a flu shot at my local pharmacy yesterday. The head pharmacist, April, is a gifted shot giver. She has you sit in a chair, and there is a pretty picture of a beach on the wall for you to look at while she sticks the needle with the stinging vaccine in your arm. That's not what I mean by commendation. Sincere commendation means pointing out where people are currently growing in their faith, living out the way of discipleship, and inviting others to join the journey. In my teaching, the same principle comes into play. When a student preaches in class, an activity that brings with it lots of anxiety, I don't just immediately list all the things that could have been better. I begin by talking about strengths, because there are always some of those. Only after we discuss what went well do we move into a discussion of "strengtheners." The preacher who habitually engages in negative stereotyping doesn't think to commend her people.

Underestimation Becomes Education

The shift from underestimation to respectful education is a continual process. I find it helpful to state the positive perspective in the form of a first-person pledge from the preacher to the congregation:

- I care enough to get to know you and to allow that knowledge to inform every sermon.
- I know your names. I know what you do for a living. I know what you're interested in. I know your politics. I know where you go to school. I know what music you're listening to, what movies and TV shows you're watching, and what blogs you're reading. I know what you are wondering about. I know your anxieties and your hopes. I know your losses and your gains. I know your ages and your stages.
- I care enough to research your questions about life and faith.

- I care enough to teach you something in every sermon.
- I care enough to engage your interest in every sermon.
- I care enough to offer you good news in every sermon, with its distinctive blend of comfort and challenge.
- I respect you enough to honor your privacy, to acknowledge that I don't know just how you feel.
- I respect you enough to learn from you every week and to allow that to inform my sermons. I learn from your wisdom, your faith, and your knowledge.

Compartmentalization Becomes Unification

Preach to the whole person in every sermon—mind, heart, and will. Preach to your listeners' intellect. Teach them something in every sermon. Preach to the will. Hold listeners, including yourself as the preacher, accountable to act on the word that is preached.

It takes both reason and emotion to motivate someone to action, however, so preach to your listeners' emotions. The word *emotion* comes from the Latin verb *movere*, "to move." The role of emotion in motivation is like the action of spark plugs in a car. Gasoline may enter a combustion chamber, but without the spark igniting the process, nothing happens. Emotions are active feelings. We experience them in relation to someone or something. That's why abstractions rarely stir emotions. They are too distant and conceptual (Hogan and Reid 1999, 75).

After a chapter that has offered a neat typology, I must confess that I know full well that typologies are always simpler than real life. I know full well that the transition from what not to say to what to say about our people is a lifelong process. The same is true, I suppose, of every aspect of preaching. We make progress, and we backslide.

But, thank God, there is always next week.

Questions for Reflection

1. Have I made as much effort to exegete my congregation as I have my text?
2. Do I know their questions, concerns, and cultural context?
3. Have I used jargon or technical language that will distance me from them?
4. Is the sermon colored by any general negative assumption I hold about my congregation?

5. Do any of my illustrations convey negative stereotypes about a particular group of people?
6. Does the sermon show my respect for the uniqueness and mystery of the congregation's experiences, as a community and as individuals?
7. Does this week's sermon in some way represent a refreshing change from last week's?
8. Does my sermon respect the congregation's hunger for biblical and theological knowledge, presented in a clear and engaging way? Does it teach them something?
9. Does the sermon tell the truth of the Gospel, not a domesticated version I assume the congregation would prefer to hear?
10. Is there something in the sermon that addresses the mind, the heart, and the will?
11. Is the sermon heavy on abstractions without illustration?
12. Is the sermon boring?
13. Is the emotional response the sermon encourages in keeping with the Gospel?
14. Does the sermon point people not just toward their obligations but toward the power of God that alone can assist us in fulfilling those obligations?

Chapter 5

What Not to Say (and What to Say) in the Middle

In the middle of difficulty lies opportunity.

Albert Einstein

In the middle of a sermon lies difficulty.

John Holbert (among many others)

The human story does not always unfold like a mathematical calcula-tion on the principle that two and two make four. Sometimes in life they make five or minus three; and sometimes the black board topples down in the middle of the sum and leaves the class in disorder and the pedagogue with a black eye.

Winston Churchill

Beginnings are usually scary and endings are usually sad, but it's the middle that counts. You have to remember this when you find yourself at the beginning.

Sandra Bullock, actress

I think it is fair to say that more sermons go off the rails, crash and burn, plod into chaos, and leave listeners in the lurch somewhere in the middle. A rivet-ing and promising beginning and a potent and memorable end seem easier to create than all that stuff in the middle. This chapter is about how to get from beginning to ending without lulling the hearers to sleep, without confusing the hearers into catatonia, without, once again, driving the hearers to take up the hymnal and count just how many tunes they know. Sandra Bullock is spot on with her comment: it is finally the middle that counts.

But the quote by Churchill needs attention too. He certainly did not have sermons in mind when he spoke of the messiness of the human story, but since we do, we do well to remember that all the skills and tricks we may use to keep the attention of hearers have a way of failing despite our best efforts. It is not always our fault when listeners take their minds elsewhere: the lunch to come, the surgery that looms, the feverish child, the humming pew mate, and the preacher's shoes all have a hand in dragging ears to distant lands. More than a few sermons I have preached and heard have collapsed on themselves, leaving the hearers disconnected and the preacher with the homiletical equivalent of a black eye.

That said, there are things we can do to mitigate the ear loss. There are ways to make useful and helpful connections in the middle of sermons so as to keep our hearers with us, at least so far as the above distractions, and a thousand others, make it possible. But as we have done again and again in this book, we will first look at some ways we in our preaching have nearly forced our congregations to stop listening. God knows that we do not wish to jettison our parishioners, but God also knows that we do too often leave them behind, like washing dirt off cars, plucking hairs from our brows, or tossing trash in the bin. Just what have we said and done in the middle of our sermons that has slammed ears shut like an enraged teenager's bedroom door?

What Not to Say in the Middle

That Hoary Old Friend: Three Points and a Poem

Preachers for centuries have relied on some form to order what they propose to say. Ancient folklore points to the "rule of three" that has long structured many a tale: "The Three Billy Goats Gruff," "The Three Little Pigs," "Three Blind Mice." There is an emotional wholeness locked into a phrase that announces, "this, this, and this." When the theological notion of the Trinity in Christian theology is added, the idea of three seems well-nigh rooted in the foundations of the universe. However true that may be, the structuring mechanism of "three points" is riddled with danger.

Whether we call the segments of the sermon "points" or "moves" or "steps" or "pieces" or "chunks" or "episodes" or "units" or "parts," to focus on them alone is to make a crucial mistake. If I think only of the ordering of my "points," whether this story precedes that quote or follows that word study, I will have overlooked something absolutely essential: Just how do these pieces connect? What is the glue that molds them together? How does the preacher move from idea to idea without being left merely with disparate "points"? Right here is the problem with three points and poem: it is rarely nothing else than three sermons with a sadly disconnected ending.

When the preacher thinks only of the sermon's "building blocks" (still another metaphor for "points"), she resorts to numerals ("The second thing I want to say . . .") or vague connectors ("The next thing we need to look at . . .") or, perhaps worst of all, some weak time designation ("In conclusion . . ." or "If you have heard nothing I have said up to now, then listen to this" or "You have been a good congregation, so as I wrap this up . . . ," implying that listening to my sermon today has been like a dose of castor oil or eating your vegetables) in order to stick the sermon together. Sermons that use such designations to move from idea to idea do not at all help hearers hang in there. And this is so for the following simple but often overlooked fact: the preacher knows where she is going, but the congregation does not. She then concludes that she must find ways to pull the hearers by the ears if they are going to stay in the sermon with her. It is these "pulls" that we need to address. Thomas Long has a helpful metaphor of the sermon as "a long corridor with a set of doors leading to separate rooms, much like a school hallway." He urges us to "think through what happens 'out in the hallway,'" what has traditionally been called "transitions" (Long 2005, 147–48). My "ear pulls" are Long's attention to the corridors of his sermonic school hallway. I like my metaphor a bit better since it is more active; ear pulls are something I need to do as a preacher.

In chapter 3, I used an example of a beginning of one of my sermons on Joel: "Locusts are the Rambos of the insect world." I noted there that this beginning was poor for several reasons, but perhaps the worst problem was that it promised something that it could not and did not deliver, namely, some etymological details that might somehow aid our understanding of the passage from Joel. And because the sermon strode off in very different directions, there was little that I could do to connect the beginning with what followed. Hence, this startling opener remained a bleeding chunk, disconnected to the remainder of the sermon. I frankly cannot remember just how I got from that beginning to the next bit, but I am sure that it was something lame: "But of course Joel was not really talking about locusts, was he?" or "The first thing we need to know about locusts is . . ." I needed some "ear pull" to make my move from that awful opener to the middle, but the sentence was so bad that perhaps even the finest pull could not have saved it.

Using numbers or familiar adverbs of time (next, now) *to attempt to move along in the sermon runs a dual risk.* First, it may ensure that the first idea expressed will be quickly forgotten after we have moved to another one. "My second point" suggests that we have exhausted the first (which we clearly have not), and many in the congregation will hit the delete button on whatever they have been able to glean from point one. Second, certain wags in the congregation will think quickly to themselves, "He always uses three points, so that is one down and two to go—thank God!" This thought is accompanied by a glance at the watch, calculating how long this sermonic experience still has to continue: "Let's see, about five minutes per point, two points to go, plus three minutes for the poem—only about 13 minutes to survive now. May God be with me!" This sort of signaling does not help the hearer to focus on what you are saying, but on the length of your saying it. These attempts at connections are not finally ear pulls, tugging the hearers along in the logic of the sermon's content. They are rather poor attempts to glue the bits together, more Elmer's than super glue, I fear.

The poem at the end (or the hymn text or the concluding story) is too often designed to summarize the basic claim of the sermon. "Surely there is nothing wrong with that," you may say. "Is it not important to focus clearly once again on the idea of the day?" And I quickly reply, "Indeed it is!" However, unless the ear pulls of the sermon have been made clearly and well, no summarizing poem, hymn, or tale will be able to pull the fat out of the fire of the rest of the sermon. If I have used only numerals or weak adverbs of time to attempt to shove my sermon along toward some end, the poem will not be able to summarize what has not been consistently stated up to its reading. In short, you cannot summarize what the hearers have not been able to understand!

An example: Today's sermon is "You Know the Heart of a Stranger," and the text is Deuteronomy 10:12–22. The goal of the sermon is to help my congregation see that Israel struggled throughout its history with an identity that moved between the twin poles of unique and specially chosen by God on the one hand, and the necessity of opening themselves up to the world in mission on the other. The latter was in fact the very meaning of the former. In addition, I want the congregation to see that their own nation, the United States, has throughout its long history struggled in precisely the same way toward this complex identity: special somehow, but with that specialness lived out not in arrogance but in service.

This sermon is taking on some very large tasks. It will be important to order it well as I attempt to carry my hearers through my thinking on this subject that is both political and religious at the same time. Watch as three (or four!) points and a poem rears its ancient head (I telescope the example for reasons of space).

> Every nation struggles to project an identity. When I say, "France," many
> ideas may come to mind: great food, delicate wines, romance. But recently,
> when France was out of favor with some in the world, "french fries" became

"freedom fries" in some restaurants. Identities are ever changing. Think of Germany at the beginning and middle of the twentieth century. Now think of Germany in the twenty-first century. Its identity is certainly different: economic power, great beer, lederhosen, magnificent scenery.

Now think of ancient Israel. [But why should I when I am still trying to get my head around contemporary France and Germany?] It too was in the business of creating an identity. It constantly reminded itself that it spent a very long time in slavery in Egypt while it also announced that God had specially chosen it to have a unique relationship to God. Israel was to be "a kingdom of priests and a holy nation," as Exodus 19 puts it, because the power of God had lifted the Israelites out of slavery and given them a land designed just for them.

But do you see dangers lurking here? [What exactly is "here"?] How can I be both slave and chosen? What does it mean to be a chosen slave now free? What am I to do now? This leads us to our third idea. [It does? But exactly what was the second one?] The Israelites remembered that they were once slaves, and that memory is crucial. That memory prevents them from becoming slave masters once they have been granted their freedom by God. Instead of becoming oppressors, as the Egyptians were to them, they are called by God to love the stranger, precisely because they themselves know the heart of the stranger, having been strangers themselves in their own history.

And is this same concern not our own in the United States of America? [Just exactly what is that "concern"?]. Do we not fancy ourselves as unique and chosen people? Does the earliest document attributed to our ancestors, the Mayflower Compact, not describe the new settlers from Britain as "a city set on a hill," employing distinctly biblical imagery? And have we not too often denied that uniqueness by denying women the right to vote; declaring that an African American counts only as two-thirds of a person, and then cutting African Americans out of our so-called free society for centuries; decimating the first dwellers in these lands, the Native Americans, and consigning them to poverty on dry reservations? How can we be both representatives of the God of freedom and harsh oppressors of so many of our brothers and sisters?

We must always remember [here comes the summary!] the words of that great hymn written by Bishop Gerald Kennedy. Let us sing like we mean it! "God of love and God of power, thou hast called us for this hour." [But to what have we been called?]

There is a sermon in here and perhaps an effective one. But what is missing? Why does it not cohere as it should? The answer is ear pulls. Now let us examine what we need to say in the middle.

What to Say in the Middle

The Crucial Need of the Ear Pull

Ear pulls are designed to close off each segment of the sermon. By doing this task I reassure my hearers that they can follow what I am doing, and I reassure myself that I know where I am going. Never underestimate the importance of either goal!

To return to the above example, the first section was designed to introduce the subject of national identities, how nations both create images of themselves and are given images by other nations' perceptions of them. But I cannot merely point to modern perceptions of two nations' identities alone to introduce this sermon properly. I need to use the introduction more fully to get to the subject of the sermon. That subject is not merely national identity; it is the complexity of national identities and the dangers of not seeing that complexity in the light of God's desires for all nations. Hence, I must find an ear pull to fulfill the promise of the beginning. How about at the end of the opening paragraph? "But nations not only have identities that change; they also have grand hopes and dreams for themselves that they might become great nations that include all their citizens in those hopes and dreams. No nation survives for long if significant numbers of its people feel incapable of having full and rich lives in that nation." That better sets the subject of the sermon, I think. But now what?

My next ear pull is designed to help the hearers move to the next section by indicating how what is coming is related to what we have just concluded. (Note: I do not need numbers or vague "nexts" to do this.) Perhaps I can begin the next section about ancient Israel as follows: "National identity is not only a modern problem. Ancient Israel was also attempting to create a national identity as God had called it to do from the very beginning of its existence as a nation. And that struggle for identity was just as complex as any modern national struggle." You can see that only one or two sentences at the seams of the sermon can provide that missing coherence hearers long for. You really need no more than one or two sentences. More than that becomes burdensome, overloading the connector, the ear pull, making it thicker and more obvious than it needs to be. Ear pulls at the junctions of the sermon may take any one of the following shapes: (1) a simple "and" that in fact means much more like "again" or "besides" or "in addition"; (2) contrasting words such as "but," "yet," "despite," "still," or "on the other hand"; or (3) the logically based "if . . . then" and its close relations "because," "since," "thus," or "therefore."

Not only does this ear pull demonstrate how the new section relates to the one before, but it also anticipates what is about to be heard in the next section. In short, it connects and foresees at the same time. I think my three-sentence addition above does both of those tasks.

I would suggest that you, the reader, now test your own skills by adding appropriate ear pulls to the other sections of my sample sermon to glue it more clearly and tightly together. Remember that the goal of all ear pulls is simple: to tug your hearers' ears in the direction you wish them to go, namely, the direction you have designed your sermon to go. Do not force them to make up their own connectors, because they will not do so. It is not that they dislike you, and it is not that they just do not want to listen to you today (though God knows, and so do they, that some days it is plainly difficult to sustain attention, no matter how brilliant your words may be). Listening to a serious speech for fifteen minutes or so is not easy in a culture where sound bites rule the day. They need and want your help to keep up and keep engaged. So attend to those ear pulls! They are your dear friends. If you use them well, congregations will be able to hear you by being able to follow you. They may well rise up and call you blessed! Or at least they may not rise up and call you other things that ought not be uttered in church or anywhere else.

Think More Carefully about the Form You Will Use

Sermon form is much more than a random decision the preacher makes after she has gotten up some juicy content. That old friend I just made sport of above—three points and a poem—has hardly disappeared from our modern pulpits. Such a sermon form implies that only the content has been seriously considered while the form has been employed as a container in which that content may be poured after it has been appropriately mixed. When the preacher announces that "this text reminds us of three things we all should know," you can bet that the old wineskin of a very familiar form, tried and only occasionally true, cracked and barely serviceable, has once again been used to carry the hoped-for new wine in its ancient leather pouch.

But form is clearly a theological issue every bit as much as a practical one. A sermon cannot be thought of as form and content, as if they were two separate entities. We must rather speak of the form of the content, because these two things must work well together if the sermon is to be effective. For the purposes of this chapter, the choice of form will profoundly affect the movements in the middle. Let's examine briefly some possible forms for a sermon and what roles each form has on the sermon's middle.

The traditional form of three points and a poem

You see, I am not completely against such a form, and it would make little difference if I were, since you would use it anyway, wouldn't you? Such a form especially needs the device of the ear pull in order to avoid the appearance of three sermons rather than the stated goal of three ideas illustrating only one. This can be done, but the movement from point to point must be handled very carefully and with effective ear pulls to guide the listener from one to the other.

A problem-solving form

Fred Craddock, the dean of modern homiletics, suggests in his landmark book *As One Without Authority* that preachers should preach in the same way that they listen and study the biblical text. That is, when preachers read biblical texts, they are at first not aware what those texts mean. They tease the meanings out, assembling the text's clues until the meaning for this reading emerges. They should preach exactly like that. They should present in their sermon that same inductive movement, from "What might this text mean?" to "What might it mean for us today?" Such a movement could make the ear pulls rather easier, since all I am doing is replicating my own discovery process. I need only lead my hearers as I was led.

The Lowry loop

Eugene Lowry proposed in 1980 his "loop," a sermon movement based on the "one essential" element in any sermon: ambiguity (Lowry 1980, 76). A sermon must begin in ambiguity, a problem that energizes and troubles the hearer. Then that problem must be explored and articulated to convince the hearer that it is a serious problem of contemporary human existence. Then the preacher must hint at the clue to the resolution of the problem; this should take the form of a "sudden illumination" from the Gospel. That illumination is then made clearer and fuller just before the implications are teased out for what can now be done as a result of this Gospel, or at least what it is now possible to do. Again, with this very determinative shape, the ear pulls should be obvious as long as the five components are seen in their proper relationships to one another: the problem is presented, then explored, then shown to be solvable, then solved more fully, then the implications for us delineated and celebrated.

The mind as camera

David Buttrick employs the metaphor of a camera to describe the way in which all sermons should move (Buttrick 1987). In the same way that a camera captures images, using a wide variety of lenses, creating foreground and background, so our minds work in the same way. As the camera shutter opens, the image is captured, and then the shutter closes and moves to the next frame. Buttrick claims this image will greatly help preachers as they order their material in the sermon. The first idea is presented as the preacher opens the hearers' lenses, but before moving to the next frame, the preacher closes that first frame down. The camera cannot offer clear single pictures unless the shutter opens and closes; if it does not, the pictures will be blurred together. In this model the ear pulls are very clear. I present the idea in one clear statement in order that the hearer may take a picture of it and get that idea in mind. I then develop that one idea by clarifying it, developing it, or raising objections to it, depending on the needs of the sermon. Then, and most importantly, I close this idea down by restating it, thus announcing that it is complete; the shutter of the camera has closed and we are ready to move to the next idea. For Buttrick, no sermon can offer more than five or six of these moves, and each move can be no more than about four minutes long if the hearer is to be able to maintain connection to the sermon.

Many other forms are surely possible. The crucial thing, however, is to pay the most careful attention to the ear pulls in the middle no matter what form your sermon takes. Without such attention, the sermon will not maintain its interest for the hearer, and the hope for the sermon, the powerful proclamation of the Gospel, will be lost. Fortunately, ear pulls are easy to use the more you pay attention to them and the more you practice them. No one first steps into a pulpit knowing about the central need for ear pulls, but glazed eyes, inattentive and slumped bodies, and furtive glances at timekeeping devices will tell the alert preacher that the ear pulls, along with Elvis, have left the building.

Miscellaneous Bits about the Middle

I have listened to and preached thousands of sermons in a career that has now spanned forty years or so, and I have heard (and spoken) any number of what might be called "preacherly affectations." These are profoundly irritating ticks or barnacles that need to be burned off or scraped off (depending on the metaphor) to make possible the clear hearing of our sermons. I will now list some.

Unpleasant speech bits

Beware of falling into speech patterns like "Don't cha know?" (very affected) or "In any case" (witheringly boring) or the ever popular "ya know," designed to drive hearers insane and demonstrate beyond doubt that the preacher is an idiot and can think of little valuable to say. Any repeated speech bits like these are the homiletical equivalent of constant swearing in everyday speech. People use "F-bombs," "S-explosives," and other verbal (perhaps preverbal is closer to it) incendiary devices because they just can't think of anything else to say. To quote a famous book title, we live in a "confederacy of dunces." And continuous use of such unpleasant speech bits will make you eligible to join the confederacy. These bits are a poor attempt to connect sermons by saying the same things over and over again, however mindlessly. Such bits do not connect anything, save "fool" and "preacher" in the hearer's minds.

Stained-glass voice and its companion, aw shucks voice

In the early days of the twentieth century, and certainly in the nineteenth, stained-glass voice was an occupational hazard for preachers. If one had little to say, one could at least say it in such a way that was thought to be pro-foundly and sonorously religious. You know the voice I mean. It is employed at least an octave below the natural pitch of the voice, the consonants and vowels are chiseled and explode from the mouth and tongue, and the great word "God" is uttered in multiple syllables. And it sounds phony, inevitably, because it is. This was often a male problem, but now that I have heard many female preachers, I've concluded that stained-glass voice is a gender-neutral problem. Be yourself in the pulpit. Just talk like you talk, and if you have a sort of stained-glass voice, well, use it carefully, being certain to make clear that you just can't help it.

Aw shucks voice is the more difficult problem in today's pulpits, I think. Preachers no longer wish to sound the way preachers have been thought to sound over the centuries. Instead, they just want to sound like real people. As we say here in the South, "Aw shucks. I'm jist one o' y'all." I am too often reminded of that terrible old TV show *Hee Haw*, where every performer tried to out twang the other for an hour every week. They all came off as corn-pone, grit-lovin' hicks, and that was apparently the point. The show implied that real people like corn pone and grits, washed down with moonshine liquor, and some preachers I hear in my classes and in the pulpits surround-ing my seminary lay their hickness on with a trowel. Let me be clear. I like accents; they show that we are not all the same. Because I have long vocal training, when I preach in the pulpits of the South, I am often thought to have been born in England; I sound downright "posh," even dreadfully affected, to some people around here! I always tell my students that accents are only a problem if they detract from what they are trying to say. Just don't "put it on," whichever "it" you have.

Drama king or queen

Not all parts of your sermon are generated with the same emotional intensity. If you shout or speak very loudly all the time, ears will first shut off and then their owners will look for the nearest exit. This is true in every preaching tradition. The old African American phrase "Start slow, go higher, strike fire" is not a bad one to remember. But even that should not be the constant pattern. Anything you do in the pulpit again and again will become over time the source of boredom and finally ridicule. When the youth sit in the balcony and count the number of times you say or do a certain thing, it is time to take stock of your preaching patterns. Human emotions are multiple; try to use more than one of them in your preaching.

Tear-jerking stories

We have spoken elsewhere about the dangers of an overly emotional story at the beginning and end of the sermon, but the danger lurks in the middle too. Some hearers feel so good after they have had a cry, they just wait for the preacher to drag them to the weeper's bench. But the goal of our preaching is not to make our hearers cry. Genuine emotion can be a wonderful thing and can indeed lead believers to a closer relationship to God, but very emotional stories can just as easily be signs of homiletical manipulation. Such emotional finagling does not lead to God but to the dangers of a false piety, watered in tears rather than in true feeling.

How Many Parts Should a Sermon Have, and How Long Should It Be?

Attention spans have certainly shortened in the past few decades. Some have called us the "Sesame Street culture"—give us information in small bites and give it to us fast and cute. How else can one explain the huge success of *USA Today*, known by some in the newspaper business as "MacPaper"? People simply no longer are interested in receiving information in long gulps. These are facts.

Yet they are to some extent secular and ethnocentric facts. The church is, after all, the church, and it has its own set of listening expectations that exist apart from *Sesame Street* and *USA Today*. When people come to church, they anticipate hearing a discourse of some length that will test their willingness to listen over some course of time. And if they are in certain ethnic churches (African, African American, or Latino/Latina), their expectations often anticipate rather longer sermons, occasionally up to and exceeding one hour. Such longer sermons are regularly punctuated with call and response, in which the congregation is deeply engaged in the listening and the creation of the preaching event. I worshiped in an African American congregation for two years, and this experience suggested to me that while *Sesame Street* may have been a favorite show, its attention span diminution was little in evidence. Sermons in this church were seldom if ever shorter than forty minutes.

Still, it is important to recognize that the ears of our hearers have been changed by culture and to think carefully about how those changes might affect the listening of sermons. David Buttrick has thought about these matters perhaps more carefully than the rest of us. In his huge introduction to preaching, *Homiletic*, he makes very specific demands on preachers concerning both the length of their sermons and the number of sections each sermon must have in the twenty-first century. He calls each section of a sermon a "move" (to avoid the many construction metaphors that he thinks have crippled right thinking about sermons). Each move of a sermon must have three indispensable parts: an opening statement, a development of that one idea, and a definite closure. Each of these moves can be no longer than four minutes, so a twenty-minute sermon can have no more than five or six (preferably five) of the artfully designed moves. (Buttrick's entire book is dedicated to the explication of his belief in the correctness of his theories of sermon construction and form, but pp. 294–321 provide some helpful summaries.)

Though Buttrick's theory may be overly schematic and not attentive enough to the many more poetic ways that sermons may be heard and be effective (see Long 2005, 104), we learn from him that the ways we shape our sermons, the ways that we move from idea to idea, the ways that we make what we have to say unified and coherent, are far more than incidental to the task of preaching. In fact, the shape and movement of a sermon are theological and ethical matters, not mere technical ones. If all my sermons follow one pattern (old "three points" may be in the wings again, awaiting his cue), I train my congregation to learn that the faith they have come to hear about in my sermon is formed in only one way, namely, through points and ideas alone. But that is hardly true, as any believer knows. When I attend a funeral and the great Isaac Watts hymn "O God, Our Help in Ages Past" is sung, why is it that I cannot sing it due to the tears in my voice? Is this because of ideas? Not completely, of course. So it is with sermons; their ideas may not always be the stuff that moves a hearer to a deeper connection with God.

But beware what lies in the middle, and attend to the wisdom of Sandra Bullock: "It's what's in the middle that counts." If you do not attend to the material that lies in the middle, its shape and its movement, you may have a sermon that resembles two slices of bread resting one on top of the other. But the sandwich maker has forgotten the lettuce, the mustard, the tomato, the cheese, the turkey, the ham. Two slices of bread do not a sandwich make, nor do scintillating beginnings, flabby middles, and startling ends make a sermon. What they do make are frustrated listeners whose ears have gone on an early vacation, heading for the cafeteria before the hour of worship has run its course.

Questions for Reflection

1. In using the old "three points and a poem" model, am I actually making three different, unrelated points—in effect, stringing together three different sermons?
2. Have I lost people's attention in the middle because the sermon has no way of keeping them engaged at each transition point?
3. Have I adopted preacherly affectations like "stained-glass voice" or "aw shucks voice"?
4. Is my sermon full of distracting and lazy phrases such as "ya know," or "don't cha know," or "in any case" (pick your own)? Are the youth likely to be counting how many times I've used these, and have the adults stopped paying attention to what I'm trying to say?
5. Have I maintained the same emotional tone throughout, never varying the intensity so that people are either bored with my monotony or tired out by my false intensity?
6. Have I told tear-jerking tales designed to "make 'em all cry" that too often make 'em all forget what I've been trying to say?
7. Have I closed off each sermon segment before going on to the next?
8. Have I employed "ear pulls" at the transitions of my sermon so people stay engaged?
9. Have I limited my sermon to no more than five or fewer segments and tied each one to the next with effective ear pulls?
10. Have I paid careful attention to the form of my sermon and not divorced that form from the content?

Chapter 6

What Not to Say (and What to Say) about Yourself

Oh, wad some power the giftie gie us,
To see oursels as ithers see us!

Robert Burns, "To a Louse"

What then is Apollos? What is Paul? Servants through whom you came to believe, as the Lord assigned to each. I planted, Apollos watered, but God gave the growth.

1 Cor. 3:5–6

Now I should remind you, brothers and sisters, of the good news that I proclaimed to you, which you in turn received, in which also you stand, through which also you are being saved, if you hold firmly to the message that I proclaimed to you.

1 Cor. 15:1–2

He was like a cock who thought the sun had risen to hear him crow.
George Eliot, Adam Bede

Self-love is the greatest of all flatterers.

La Rochefoucauld

*T*here is a substantial literature in homiletics concerning the use of the preacher's own life and experience in preaching (e.g., Mulligan and Allen 2005; Ramsey 2000; Switzer 1979; Thulin 1989). This is so because the issue is torn with controversy. There are obviously two general sides in the debate: never do it (Buttrick) and do it with care (nearly everyone else). I fall in the latter camp and think that Buttrick is simply off base when he denies to preachers one of the major sources of their connection with God, namely, their own lives as resources for their sermons. Our personal lives and our

76

ministerial experiences are rich fodder for preaching. However, fodder may be valuable as vitamin sources or it may be sugary treats that smell and taste grand but do the health and digestion real harm. Just how do we separate the good calories from the empty ones?

The issue is an old one, as the two quotations from the apostle Paul, from the same Corinthian letter, make plain. In both cases Paul announces with no little pride that it was he who preached the word he had received, it was he who planted the Gospel in those Corinthian ears. Paul regularly uses his own conversion experience as the foundation for his evangelistic work. Indeed, as he began to preach, his former life as Christian persecutor made his conversion to the faith hard for some to believe (see especially his apology to the Galatians in 1:10–24 for that early life and his real conversion that had made him new). Thus, Paul used his own experience often in his preaching, but that experience was not always completely helpful for his proclamation. In this chapter we will explore that dilemma more fully.

What Not to Say about Yourself

Never Make Yourself the Hero or Heroine of Your Sermon

The hearer should, and finally will, become very suspicious if you describe in your sermon your latest visit to the hospital in terms like the following: "I entered the room as quietly as I could. You know how hospital rooms are; they have that certain smell—musty, closed in, laced with unknown medicines, lighted eerily, punctuated by the regular hiss of an oxygen tank or beep of a blood pressure machine. We were alone. With strange wires attached in many places, with plastic tubing running around her head and into her nose, she gazed at me and said, 'Pastor, I am so glad you are here. Thanks for coming.' I smiled and asked her to pray with me." This seems innocent enough and is familiar to any pastor. But note the implied messages: First, you are inordinately familiar with hospital rooms, suggesting that you spend enormous amounts of time there, an indication that you are indeed a wonderful pastor, available to your flock always; you are in fact a heroic hospital pastor. Second, your parishioner is monumentally glad that you have taken time from your incredibly busy schedule to grace her with your benevolent presence; things are definitely looking up for her now that you have come; you are indeed a hero. Third, because you are a deeply spiritual person, you of course ask first for prayer; God demands it, she expects it, and your congregation will relax to know that you always pray at these difficult moments; now you are a hero of prayer too.

In every way this little story of a hospital visit has cast you as the hero/ heroine. It may seem innocuous, but it misuses your pastoral work to shine the spotlight on you. Are you the subject of the sermon? Hardly. Your pastoral experience can become a vehicle for God's Grace, God's healing, a call for repentance. God is finally the subject of all our sermons, and it is to God that our experiences always must point. The apostle Paul never used his own experience, even of his crucial conversion, as a way to point to his own greatness, but rather as a way to point inexorably to the fabulous Grace of God.

You may also become the unintended hero or heroine by pretending that you are not, through that tricky fiend—false modesty: "Well, friends, you know that I do my best up here, but it is always a real struggle for me. God knows I try to preach as well as I can, but I am just a country boy with few experiences of the world, a halfway decent voice, and an average brain. When I became the pastor of this church, I felt immediately that I had risen far above my capabilities. But I just knew with God's gracious help that I would not mess you up too badly." Can you see that by speaking like this you are in fact luring people into contradicting you, pleading with them to disagree? Deeper down, you actually are convinced that you are a fabulous preacher, blessed with superb skills and deserving of any number of preaching awards, but you continually need your hearers to affirm you as such. "Aw shucks, ma'am, I am doing my best" actually means, "I know that I am good, but I need desperately for you to say it to me!" False modesty is a sign of deep insecurity, of a preacher on a slippery slope to disaster. If you are begging for adulation from your congregation, without which you cannot survive as a pastor, your motivation is seriously flawed. You work for God, not for human flattery.

Then there is the public prophet who cannot wait to describe his latest foray into the jaws of oppressive structures: "During yesterday's march against our reckless government's plan to blockade the island of Tonga, I stood in the front of the line helping to hold the sign that read, 'No blood for coconuts!' Paul's great line echoed in my head: 'Woe to me if I do not proclaim the Gospel!'" Laypeople want their pastor involved in important matters of the day, but they do not want their pastor using her "heroism" as a human model for their behavior. Again, the sermon is not about you! Perhaps we preachers should tattoo that line on our foreheads: "The sermon is not about us; it is about God."

Do Not Share Intimate Material in a Sermon

I actually cringe as I write this, for I have heard too many sermons in which the preacher has shared more of himself than he ought. I can guess why.

Many famous preachers have reached into the storehouse of their past and uncovered difficult experiences of alcoholism, drug abuse, sexual promiscuity, pornographic addiction, abusive relationships, among many other human activities, and then have used these as contrasts for their current, transformed lives. Such preaching, "I once was lost, but now am found," has a venerable history. But there are dangers here.

We live in a culture that is overly interested in the lives of others. So-called reality shows dot our TVs, programs that focus on the very intimate lives of human beings who apparently are willing to expose their personal selves to a wide viewing audience in ways that a generation ago would have been unthinkable. Just today, I watched a video of a program called *Housewives of New Jersey*. In this video, five women, all of whom are married and living in the same New Jersey neighborhood, end an evening together by assaulting one another verbally in expletive-deleted fashion, attempting, I think, to win some sort of prize as the most desperate housewife of them all. It was a remarkable display of unbridled fury, laced with language that was in earlier days confined to the privacy of only the most dysfunctional homes.

Your congregation is without doubt quite fascinated by your private life, but that is not altogether a healthy interest. An example from my experience: A pastor had had a divorce from his first wife just before being assigned to another pastoral post. Soon after his arrival, he married again and found himself blissfully happy with his second wife and the two children she brought with her to this, her second marriage. The congregation was very pleased that their pastor found his new married state so fulfilling. Unfortunately, he spoke of his joy incessantly, regularly contrasting his present happiness with the very sad life he had been living with his first wife. His new wife sat in the front pew, gazing adoringly at her new husband as he described the horror of his first marriage.

This example is inappropriate in several ways: (1) It denigrates a woman who is not available to defend herself from what is actually calumny; (2) it creates a portrait of marital bliss that is probably a bit unreal; (3) it plays into the peering desires of a voyeuristic culture; and (4) perhaps most damagingly, it shows that the pastor is all too ready to speak of the most intimate details of his life. What other matters, his hearers may think, will he feel free to speak of publicly. Will their revelations to him in the pastoral study become fodder for a sermon before another congregation?

This example is so egregious that you might think you would never do anything like that. But what about this? "In my former life I was a personal financial counselor. My sole goal was to make money for my clients and, of course, make a wad of cash for myself. And I was very good at this work. I had the big house, the swimming pool, three luxury cars, and regularly flew off, business class, to various exotic vacation spots. But I finally found all that empty somehow. Since I have been a pastor, without all those things—those things the world said we all should want—I have never been happier. My small parsonage, my Toyota hybrid, and my family vacations, are all I need. I thank God each day for the second chance I have to discover all the genuine gifts that life has to offer."

What are the perils here? First, "Lord, it's hard to be humble" comes to mind! This pastor's message could be summarized this way: "I once was rich, and I could be again, but I have chosen to devote myself to you, my beloved flock. And I am very happy to do so." This pastor is focused on self. "Be like me," she screams, "because I have found the very key to the fulfilled life." This sermon is not about God at all. Second, the pastor is the heroine of the sermon. She has given up the "good life" to "suffer for the Gospel." A Toyota is hardly a hair shirt or a crown of thorns, but compared to a Lamborghini, which she once had, her "sacrifice" is offered as proof of near-martyrdom. La Rochefoucauld had it right: "Self-love is the greatest of all flatterers." And, it could be added, also the greatest of all deceivers.

Take one more example: "I once spoke to a woman in one of my previous churches who shared with me a very personal problem, one she had not revealed to anyone. I was very uncomfortable as she talked with me, since it was a problem that I knew something about and had struggled with on several other occasions. As she spoke about the problem, I silently asked God for strength so that I might be helpful to her. Do you call on God when you are confronted with a painful difficulty?"

The example again may seem innocuous, but land mines are hidden close to the surface. First, however vaguely the pastor speaks of a conversation from a previous parish, he announces to his present congregation that he is ready to employ private conversations as sermonic material. Private conversations are just that: private and confidential. *Never* use such conversations publicly, no matter how well you think you are disguising them. Second, by employing such an illustration, the pastor is saying that he has entry into very private matters, because he is a deeply trustworthy person. Unfortunately, the fact that he has now employed one such conversation in a sermon suggests that his trustworthiness is of very limited value. In short, he is no one to be trusted. Third, the preacher is a tease. His multiple use of the word "problem" sets the minds of his hearers chattering: what sort of problem was this? Fourth, the preacher intended to use this illustration to say that we should all call on God when we face problems we cannot face alone—surely a helpful thing for a preacher to say—but this was a very ill-chosen way to get at that issue. By the time that the preacher got to God, the difficulties of the story had swamped any value that the God reference might have had.

Do Not Use Detailed Personal Experiences Very Often

In a time when narrative preaching is a powerful and prominent homiletical device, the use of personal experiences, the stories that make up a preacher's life, can be seductive. After all, one may think, I am like my parishioners in many ways. I sleep in a bedroom, eat in a kitchen, brush my teeth in a bathroom, mow my lawn, take vacations, work on my car, play golf, work with wood, and so on. Surely, the activities of my life can become revelatory of the presence and power of God, and by using these regularized events as stories that reveal God, I invite my hearers to become "detectives of divinity," opening their eyes to witness God's presence in their own common experiences.

In theory, there is really nothing wrong in employing the preacher's experiences in this way: "I had a dream last night"; "There is something very satisfying about working on your own car"; "The Grand Canyon is magnificent beyond all telling"; "Have you ever added up the number of times you have brushed your teeth in your life?"; "What a delight it is to watch a piece of wood emerge as a butterfly under the actions of your own chisel." Any of these sentences could serve well as an entry into an exploration of the power of God in our lives. But again there are dangers.

A steady diet of one's own experiences can leave a congregation bored. Without realizing it, the preacher can become Uncle Ted, that relative who comes to the family reunion chock full of the stories of his year and more than ready to regale you with his latest trip to the Caymans for windsurfing with Marge, his much younger spouse. If you are especially unfortunate, Ted will have pictures to show and, if you have been especially bad, a PowerPoint presentation made up of 600 partially sorted slides, 240 of which are of Marge on her surfboard, falling into the sparkling blue water headfirst or feetfirst, screaming with delight. Constant references to the preacher's personal life transform him into an Uncle Ted, and like Uncle Ted's family, the congregation may rush swiftly for the exits. To you, your life may indeed be exciting, but "You just had to have been there" may be an important phrase to remember. Your listeners were likely not there when you saw that bear rear up, so do not become Uncle Ted and tell them about it.

Too many personal experiences may cause the congregation to wonder whether the preacher is using them for her own psychological needs. Consider the following example: "As many of you know, our family just got back from our house high in the mountains. It is so cool there, so beautiful.

The mountains were snowcapped, the trees were golden, the sky was an electric blue. I can really be myself there, let down my hair, leave my problems behind, read what I want, say what I want, eat what I want. Why, that place is well-nigh paradise for me. I just did not want to come home at all. I cried as our car found its way down that stunning mountain and back into this hot, crowded city."

Just what is this pastor's story of her trip saying? She loves it there; she does not love it here. Maybe she would prefer to be elsewhere. Maybe she needs a break from her ministry with us. This vacation story that may have been little more in the pastor's mind than a short report of her recent trip has revealed a good deal more about her state of mind than she imagined. Too much personal talk can be far more revelatory of our states of mind than we intend.

Too many personal stories can communicate to the congregation that the pastor is just lazy. I do not have to read anything to tell personal stories. I do not have to study my Bible that carefully if I can get a decent idea from it and then spin out a relevant personal story to make the point. I do not have to read any book of theology if my sermon is made up of my personal experiences. I do not have to be alert to recent findings in science or studies in sociology or actions of government or world conflicts if I only relate my personal stories to illustrate the great work of God. In short order, the members of the congregation will no longer trust their pastor to do the main thing they hope their pastor will do, namely, be their spokesperson who attempts to discover the movement of God in the world in which all of us live, not just the world in which the pastor lives. My attempts to find God in my personal life can be helpful to those who do not share in that life, but more often than not, my search for God in my life is finally that: *my* search in *my* life. I may be a model for others, but perhaps too often I am more like Uncle Ted.

Use Family Experiences Very Sparingly

It is always a great temptation to use scenes from one's own family as illustrations for sermons. Given the inordinate interest in human reality shown by modern people, and especially the realities of the pastoral family shown by a congregation, the preacher may often score a real hit by using anecdotes from the parsonage or manse. Congregations have long enjoyed the latest pratfall of the pastor's son or the most recent "darndest thing" out of the mouth of the precocious daughter. And what preacher has not revealed, often in a humorous way, a difference of opinion between herself and her mate concerning any number of family issues, from parenting, to shopping, to sports, to lawn care. Pastors employ these experiences to say to the congregation, "We are a family too, just as many of you are; we love one another, but we also have our moments." I urge you to think very carefully about using such material in your sermons.

It is often said in the homiletical literature that if preachers do use family material from the pulpit, they must get the approval of the person being discussed. However, children under the age of ten or so cannot effectively know what such public portrayals of their lives can mean for them or for their family. Their "cute" actions or words that become sermonic illustrations are at the very least embarrassing for them. I suggest that such experiences never be the source of sermonic material. And the older the child, the higher the risk of embarrassment or even humiliation. Is it not partially true that the terrible cliché of the "preacher's kid" as an exemplar of bad behavior exists as a result of the inappropriate use of the pastor's child as sermon item, adding thereby to the "fish bowl" existence that pastoral families are too often forced to live? When a preacher uses a family member, especially a child, in a sermon, the danger of caricature is always real, whether that caricature is positive or negative. I will say it plainly: never use any of your children as sermon examples.

My wife is a pastor, and she on occasion uses me in her sermons as illustration, usually of our close relationship to one another. She asks me beforehand if I mind being mentioned, and I generally say I do not mind. But I do try to weigh very carefully the possible effects that the illustration might have. I have my own life apart from the church my wife serves, and I have a strong identity apart from her. I do not mind a gentle teasing, since I am convinced that my wife loves me and would do nothing to demean or make fun of me, either privately or publicly. I have tried to nuance such sermonic use in as many ways as possible to indicate the great care that must be used if a preacher is ever to use family in a sermon. It is fair to conclude that such use should be very rare indeed.

An example from one of my past sermons: "I was driving down the highway the other day, and my three-year-old son, Darius, was strapped into his car seat in the back. Suddenly, out of the silent car, he proceeded to read an entire billboard, word for word, an advertisement of one thing or another. I almost drove off the road! I had no idea he could read, despite the fact that he and I often watched *Sesame Street* together, on occasion several times a day. When I asked him how he had done it, he said, 'I don't know, Dad. It just came to me.'" As I remember the sermon, this was an illustration of surprise that led to a discussion of the surprises of God. This family anecdote was certainly cute, it certainly revealed a precociousness on the part of my son (who was and is certainly a brainy guy), and it might very well have served as a decent illustration for that sermon. So what was wrong with it?

First, my son was three years old and hence incapable of agreeing or not to the use of the story. It reminds me of an old television show starring Art Linkletter called *Kids Say the Darndest Things*. In this show, the adult star spoke to kids, coaxing them to say things judged (by adults) as wise beyond their years. Of course, Linkletter was actually using the kids to speak to an audience filled with adults, who laughed at the verbal antics of the precocious kids. This show is not unlike many "children's" sermons I have heard that in reality are thinly disguised messages for adults that use cute kids to make the point. The kids are hardly the target of the sermon; they are the means to speak to the adults through them. This could be called church child abuse, and I would have to admit that my use of my son's experience in the car was rather like that.

Second, by telling the story of my son, and my parenting of him, I was calling attention to his brilliance, as well as my own, for being his father. So, again, although perhaps this time more subtly, the sermon holds me up as a hero, a great and wise father, who has produced a genius for a son.

Third, my hearers that day were likely to use my son's story to develop some incorrect images. Of course, I have no way of knowing, but I can imagine they told that story once or twice to friends and family, pointing out that their pastor had a son who was reading at three, which was no surprise since his father had a PhD in Hebrew Bible studies before he became a pastor and thus was himself a brilliant man. The problem with this is that it fixed in their minds a narrow and certainly incorrect notion of who I was, who my son was, who we were as father and son, and who I was as a pastor. Stories possess great power, but they can define a person in inappropriately narrow ways. I am very proud of my son, but that story limits him and me. I wish I had not used it as I did.

What to Say about Yourself

Now that I have drawn a fairly tight noose around the use of personal experience illustrations in sermons, it is time to suggest several ways that such experiences may be used that can be helpful to our hearers. Despite David Buttrick's forceful statement "To be blunt, there are virtually no good reasons to talk about ourselves from the pulpit" (Buttrick 1987, 142), the fact remains that some excellent source material for sermons comes from our own life experiences. To summarize my injunctions in the previous section, the primary problem with the use of our experiences in preaching is that we are too often the central subject of that experience. *A more appropriate use of personal experience is if we see ourselves as observers of experience, rather than primary actors.* Here are some examples.

Danish philosopher Søren Kierkegaard told of a time when he was in a cemetery in Copenhagen listening to a conversation between a young boy and his grandfather. The two of them were standing at the gravesite of the boy's father, the older man's son. The older man was telling his grandson about the wonderful man that his son, the boy's father, had been, how he had been so thoughtful, so attentive, so concerned about those who had entered his life, and how he was a man of the very profoundest faith in God. Kierkegaard concluded that he had in this experience "overheard the Gospel." He understood this to be a very important and memorable way that the Gospel can be heard—that is, "overheard" rather than being told more directly. (Fred Craddock used this experience as determinative for his own fresh understanding of the act of preaching in his 1971 book *Overhearing the Gospel.*) Kierkegaard's encounter showed him to be the observer, not the actor, and his reflection on the encounter is the stuff of the sermon. The dead man's faith and human worth, as related by the grandfather to his grandson, point to the activity of God in the deceased man's life and in the lives of those relatives still living. Preachers are privileged to observe human beings at very significant moments in their lives, and this old story can be a model for ways those observations may be illustrative of God's presence in the world.

I had an experience some twenty-five years ago not unlike Kierkegaard's. I was a congregant in a church where a man had been the business manager for many years. He was a decent man but a wary, sometimes bitter one. The church was located in the downtown of a large city and attracted to its cool and comfortable building all kinds of people, many of whom were homeless or in great need. I was coming down the hall from the direction of the sanctuary one day and witnessed the following scene: The business manager was moving down a hallway perpendicular to the one I was walking down, and at that moment a woman and a small child entered the building from the opposite direction. I saw her enter just as the man did, but the man could not see me; he clearly thought he was alone. The woman was poorly dressed and not very clean. Her child had only a T-shirt and diaper on and was also not clean. I saw the first look of the man as he saw the woman and the child. That look said," Here we go again! Another poor woman with her sad child. When will these people stop bothering us with their incessant neediness!" That look stayed for a few seconds, but it was soon replaced by a very different look. The hard and frustrated look disappeared and was replaced by one of very deep and sincere compassion. His features nearly melted as he moved toward the woman, spoke softly and tenderly to her, picked up the child and led them to the office where they could receive the help they needed. I saw the entire scene and found it a very moving one, fragrant with the Gospel. This personal experience could be used as an example of the genuine deep care that humans feel for those who have needs when they are directly confronted with them. For the business manager, this woman and child became more than just another needy family; they became God's children, fully worthy of all the care he could muster. Like Kierkegaard, I was observer here, not actor. I report the scene; I am the narrator telling the story. Note that wonderful events like this one do not need lengthy explanations or interpretations. The power of God fairly flows from such episodes; explanations tend to weaken their power rather than enhance it.

A preacher can also cast a personal story as one about a "person": "I heard of a person whose child read an entire billboard at the age of three. When the astonished father asked the child just how she had done it, the child said, "I don't know, Dad; it just came to me!" By casting this story about my own son as being about some other (unnamed) person, I remove the opportunity for the hearers to focus their attention onto me as the great father of a genius. The sermon is not about any of those things, however true or false they may be, but about the presence and power of God in our lives. Some may question this strategy: "But is that not lying to the congregation? Should you not say that you are speaking of your own child?" My response is that if I find the illustration worthy of use, I want to avoid the misuse of it by the congregation. Those people have come to hear of God, not of my parental prowess or my precocious children. Still, such criticism is not to be dismissed out of hand, so I may decide to look elsewhere for an illustration that can lead us to today's theme, thereby avoiding the possibility of deceiving my hearers or misleading them to focus on me or my family instead of God.

A preacher can present a dilemma and raise the question of her own response, or lack of response, to that dilemma: "Last week I drove toward the church and went by that man. You all know the one I mean; he is in a wheelchair, he is filthy, and he is holding a cardboard, hand-lettered sign that says, "Homeless. Need food." In the past, I lowered my window, handed him a dollar, and muttered, "God bless you," as I raised the window against the searing heat of the morning. But last week, I just went right on by without a nod or a word, saying to myself that my dollars had surely gone for drugs or booze or both and that my paltry handouts were not doing him or me any lasting good. I called the homeless shelter and spoke to someone who knew him. She said he came in when it got really hot, but he preferred being on the streets. Once I saw the police tell him to move; the city had a law against such panhandling. I did not see him for a time, but there he was again last week, in the same place with his infernal sign. I hardly know what to do! I am troubled by him, but stymied in my response. What do you think I should do? What would you do? Does our text today offer any help?" This is a personal experience, and the preacher is the main actor. But she does not make herself out to be villain or hero; she is not falsely modest or finally comfortable with her actions. She uses her own dilemma as a way into a dilemma for all of her hearers. In short, she becomes one of us in honesty and struggle with a type of person we have all seen. She names our problem and carries us into the Gospel to explore what we might do—or better, what God can do and would bid us do.

A preacher's lived experience can certainly become a vehicle for revelations of the presence and power of God. But there are dangers here. Remember George Eliot's warning, and do not become like a cock that imagines the sun has come up to hear him crow. The congregation has not rolled out of bed this Sabbath to listen to a crowing cock, but to witness a preacher pointing squarely to the rising sun of the Gospel of God.

Questions for Reflection

1. Have I made myself the hero or heroine of my stories?
2. Have I overused intimate material from my own life?
3. Have I implied that my life is grander and more meaningful than others' lives by my exclusive use of personal examples?
4. Have I overused family experiences as fodder for my sermons?
5. Have I learned to become an observer of an experience, rather than always the center of attention in an experience?
6. Have I shared with hearers my own struggles to live out the Gospel and not always presented myself in the hero or heroine role?

Chapter 7

What Not to Say (and What to Say)
in Stories

I love to tell the story, because I know 'tis true;
it satisfies my longings as nothing else can do.
                                        Katherine Hankey, 1868

*W*hen we tell people stories in our sermons, we hope that they'll lean
forward with breathless anticipation. In reality, they often roll their eyes,
cross their arms, and look at their watches. When they show signs of impa-
tience, it is because inside they are asking themselves, "Why is he telling
me this?"

So before launching into guidelines for storytelling in sermons, we need
to answer this broader question: Why tell stories at all in our sermons? There
are three kinds of reasons: theological, biblical, and anthropological. The
theological reason is because our Christian faith is an incarnational faith.
God became flesh and dwelt among us. That is a story with a plot, characters,
scenes, and a theme.

The biblical reason to tell stories is because God's creating, forgiving,
and sustaining presence with humankind takes the form of a story that arches
over the whole of Scripture and the whole of our lives. I would make the
case that every genre of Scripture (poetry, law, proverbs, prophetic oracles,
apocalyptic, Gospels, epistles) is rooted in that story.

The anthropological reason to tell stories in sermons is that people like
stories. The preaching theory of the past thirty-five years, the so-called New
Homiletic, is based on the belief that everybody is trying to make a coherent story out of the weird, disconnected jumble of experiences of our lives.
Preaching means inviting the listeners to place their stories in the story of
salvation, which gives our stories a better preface and a much more hopeful
ending. Even multitasking, live-in-the-moment postmoderns who have lost
touch with or never heard the salvation story yearn for sermons that make

some kind of sense of our lives. One thing that people across many cultures appreciate in preaching is storytelling.

So there are good theological, biblical, and anthropological reasons to use stories in preaching. Storytelling in sermons can take several shapes. It can mean a sermon that has several stories in it. It can take the form of a sermon that is one continuous story. It can refer to a sermon that has an underlying story shape for its plot, moving from a problem to its complication to its resolution.

This chapter takes the form of three don'ts with regard to stories: (1) don't tell stories for the wrong reasons; (2) don't tell the wrong stories; and (3) don't tell stories the wrong way. There will be some dos at the end as well. But first, the don'ts.

What Not to Say in Stories

Don't Tell Stories for the Wrong Reasons

Don't tell stories because you need therapy and can't afford it. Harry Emerson Fosdick, the influential mid-twentieth-century preacher from the Riverside Church in New York City, pioneered what he called the life-situation sermon. He believed that preaching is "counseling on a group basis." By that he did not mean that the congregation served as a counseling service for the preacher! Don't tell stories because you need to unburden yourself. I once went to a training session for faculty members serving as small group spiritual formation leaders. The facilitator gave this advice, "Don't get in front of a group and open a vein." Be especially wary of the story about yourself or your family that pops into your head while you're preaching. Family should not be used either as heroes or scapegoats in stories. If you have that niggling little question in your mind, "Is this appropriate?" don't tell it. Several years ago my brother (who gave me permission to tell this story) shaved off his mustache. When he sat down at the breakfast table the next morning, his three-year-old daughter looked at him with wide-eyed dismay. "Go back upstairs and shave it back on, Daddy," she told him. Apply this to telling the not-quite-appropriate story. Remember that while you can always go back later and tell a story, you cannot unsay it after you have said it.

Don't tell stories about yourself because you are a narcissist and cannot help but refer everything back to you and only you. Of course, if you realize you have this tendency, you're probably not a narcissist. But it never hurts to be on the alert. In deciding whether to tell a story, remember that while we always preach out of our own experience, we should not always preach explicitly about it. I overheard a parishioner in a church I once attended say about the pastor's sermons, "There is an awful lot of Steve in Steve's sermons" (not his real name).

Don't tell stories as a substitute for substance. Don't tell stories because you haven't taken time to do your exegesis and they are all you've got. Maybe you know that desperate feeling when it's Saturday night and, for whatever reason, you are not prepared. The room fills with the pungent smell of desperation, and the thought flits through your mind, "I know this doesn't fit the sermon or relate to the text, but it's entertaining and it's all I've got."

In his book *Pitfalls in Preaching*, Norbert V. Becker points out that although Jesus told numerous stories, no one referred to him as a storyteller. Rather, people called him "Teacher." When he related stories, it was for teaching purposes, not merely for entertainment. Analyze your stories to be sure they serve "to edify and move, not merely to entertain" (Becker 1973, 6).

I would add, though, that if your stories entertain, don't hold that against them. Don't exclude the humorous anecdote just because it's humorous. But don't include the humorous anecdote just because it's humorous either.

Don't tell stories because, deep down, you believe the poor, old, boring Bible needs your scintillating stories to enliven it. Let's disabuse ourselves of the notion that the Bible is dead and needs for us to resuscitate it with our stories. We need to wrap our souls around the truth that the Bible is alive and we need a transfusion, not the other way around.

Don't Tell the Wrong Stories

Don't tell stories that trivialize your point. Sometimes the story and images it contains have associations that are not at the same level of seriousness as the point you are trying to make. This is an art, not a science, so there is a fine line to walk here. I'm not saying that humor is never allowed. I once was preaching on Jesus' debut in Luke 4:16–30, in which Jesus' hometown folks are listening to him and nodding and thinking, "This is great. He's so eloquent and wise." Then when he starts preaching that Gentiles in the past had been a better audience for God's message than Jews, they get riled up all of a sudden and try to throw him off a cliff. What struck me in the text was how the anger must have been building since verse 23 and suddenly it bursts forth in verse 28 as his listeners put two and two together: his identity as a hometown boy who has the gall to get in their face like this.

I told of how my son and husband think it's amusing to turn the seat warmer on in the car when I'm in the passenger seat. In Texas in August you're already hot, so you don't notice it for a while, and then suddenly you jump off the seat and say, "Whoa, when did it get so hot in here?"

I think that story worked because I was trying to illustrate the seeming suddenness of the anger of Jesus' listeners that had actually been building for some time. It also, I thought, spoke to the primal place their anger hit them.

Before I use humor, though, I should ask myself, "What is my motivation for including it? Does it flatter my ego to be able to make an audience laugh? Does it compensate for something that is lacking in the sermon? Is the inclusion of humor to edify or to entertain? A lot of things make people laugh that are not the Gospel of Jesus Christ.

Still, Jesus himself used humor at times. A camel trying to fit through the eye of a needle is actually pretty funny, as is someone with a log in her eye trying to take a speck out of someone else's eye. Humor most often serves to point up the absurdity of certain human behaviors and situations. It can lower listeners' defenses when we're addressing them with a challenging word.

Maybe it works better when we're talking about us than when we're talking about God. I'm not sure. But I do recall another story I thought trivialized the preacher's theme. The preacher was talking about God's guidance of the Israelites during the wilderness wandering. He said, "My wife and I have a little dog. We're trying to train her. She is allowed to go certain places and not others. She can't get it through her head that she's not allowed on our bed. When she jumps up, we whap her with a rolled-up newspaper. In the same way, God disciplined the Israelites in the wilderness."

That to me trivializes the depth of God's mercy and justice in dealing with the Israelites. It also trivializes their identity and the moral character of their disobedience, but it's the trivializing of God that makes it not work for me.

Maybe I'm saying that we can take some liberties with pointing up the absurdity of human behavior, but we need to be more careful in the stories we tell about God. People tend to literalize what we say about God. And the picture of a God who waits to whap us with a newspaper when we jump up where we're not supposed to is not the mental image we want to send people home with.

I sometimes get into trouble because I feel compelled to fit a story into a sermon simply because it just happened to me and is fresh and, to me, interesting. That does not mean that it makes the same point as the sermon and should be included. Be suspicious of the "Oh, I just have to share this" impulse. No, you don't.

One more example: There is the now probably famous example of the preacher talking about stewardship whose sermon included a refrain of our objections to God's call to commitment: God calls and we say, "Okay, God, but I'm too young" or "Okay, God, but I'm too busy," and so forth. The dramatic conclusion was this statement: "Just remember, my friends, that God's but is the biggest but of all."

Don't tell stories that work against your point. Sometimes, without realizing it, we tell a story that has some element in it that distracts from the theme we're trying to underscore. It may even make the opposite point or a competing point from the one we're trying to make.

Suppose you are preaching on the Good Samaritan and you are trying to overturn the reasons we don't stop and help others: too busy, too afraid, too self-centered. In trying to make the point that we need to overcome our fears of helping others, here is a story not to tell: A man on a business trip to Colombia in the 1980s was riding from the airport to his hotel in a Jeep with an armed driver. They came upon a man with his hands tied behind his back and blood dripping from his brow. The driver sped up and kept going. The businessman asked the driver why he didn't stop. The driver looked at him, shook his head, and said one word: "Bandito." Now you've just reinforced what you were preaching against. We hear that and think, "There are often good reasons to be suspicious of scams and cons and not to stop and help."

Now suppose you are preaching on the text from Matthew where Peter and his brothers are fishing and Jesus comes along and calls them to follow him. You are trying to make the point that when Jesus comes into our lives, he rearranges things and creates complications, but they are on the way to a life of rewarding discipleship. So don't tell the story of a tornado that swept through town and tore up several neighborhoods but that in the aftermath, people bonded and worked together and found community. The story's central analogy is between Christ and a tornado. The tornado speaks to randomness and destruction too much to carry forward your positive point about rewarding discipleship. In comparing Jesus to a tornado, you have undercut your point.

The metaphor of a riptide or undertow comes to mind. I used to go to the Jersey Shore in the summer with my family when I was growing up. I remember times when I would be trying to swim toward the shore and would feel myself being drawn back out to sea. You have to be a strong swimmer and give it your all to prevail against a riptide. A riptide is the result of two currents of water colliding under the surface. That's exactly what happens when we tell a story that makes the opposite point to the one we're trying to make. The theme of the sermon and the theme of the story collide, and listeners struggle to keep their heads above water.

Every story that we tell in our sermons is a mini narrative. Narratives have characters, a plot that usually involves conflict, a setting, and a theme. To avoid telling stories that work against our point, we need to ask ourselves these questions before including a story in our sermon: Why am I telling them this? In other words, what is the theme of this story? If it is different from the sermon's theme, then it may sabotage the sermon. What is the purpose of telling this story? What do I hope to accomplish? Asking these questions is how we will stop ourselves before we tell a story that makes a point different from the one we were enlisting it to make.

Don't tell stories that have a different agenda from the biblical text. This is another way of saying don't use stories to promote your own agenda. Suppose you are preaching on Mark 8:31–38 ("If any want to become my followers . . .") and you tell a story of how a family in the church increased their donation to the building campaign. What is the primary reason you are telling that story? To invite others into discipleship, inspiring them that, despite its rigors, loyalty to Christ brings life? Or are you telling it to get them to give to the building campaign? I'm not suggesting that giving to the building campaign is contrary to following Christ, but is it a big enough story? Or have you shrunk the definition of discipleship so that it no longer fits the text in its theological and historical context?

Another example would be a preacher giving a sermon on "Ask, search, and knock" from Luke 11:1–13. She tells the story of a woman who had lost her job, whose marriage was rocky, and whose finances were dicey. This woman "took Scripture at its word" and asked, searched, and knocked. And she finds another job, repairs her marriage, and is on the road to financial recovery because she dared to believe that God wanted the best for her! Does that story do justice to the passage in Luke? It consists of the Lord's Prayer, the parable of the Friend at Midnight, and this passage about asking, searching, and knocking. Does the metaphor of bread in the Lord's Prayer and in the parable refer to better relationships, finances, and job security? Especially in the context of Luke, a Gospel that, more than any other, warns about boiling things down to their monetary value, does this story have the same agenda as the biblical text? Or is there some other reason the preacher is telling it?

Don't tell stories that denigrate another person or a group of people. A pastor I know serves a small rural congregation. Going to Walmart is a major source of entertainment for her. She realized recently that a lot of her examples take place at Walmart. There is nothing wrong with that. Every story needs a setting. But she also realized that many of them involve her conversations with the checkout clerks, who come across as ignorant and comical or in some way needing her superior insight. She named this as a combination of classism and elitism, repented, and doesn't tell Walmart-clerk-encounter stories anymore. How would a parishioner who was a clerk at Walmart feel about these stories? How might they reinforce the prejudices of some and undercut the pastor's credibility the next time she preaches on love of neighbor?

Don't tell stories you don't have permission to tell. This goes for church members, people in the community, friends, and family. This goes even for positive stories. There are people in your church who would immediately transfer their membership if you thanked them publicly or singled them out in a positive way. Recognition is not why they do things for the church, and they adamantly prefer to remain in the background. Despite the popularity of social network sites, some people still do not want the details of their lives broadcast to a random public. We cannot assume that just because a story shows someone in a positive light, that it's okay to tell it without that person's permission.

I've always wondered how stand-up comedians spend Thanksgiving Day. I picture them alone in a hotel room eating a room-service club sandwich, not sitting around a table with the friends and family they've humiliated in their acts all year.

Since we preachers are not stand-up comedians but proclaimers of the Gospel, we need to take care with our stories. If a story has the slightest negative connotation, be very careful about telling it. I was going to tell a story one time about the preparations I was making to get ready for a visit from a neat-freak friend: alphabetizing my spices, scrubbing the floor behind the toilet, cleaning the grungy little crumbs out of the plastic utensil holder in the kitchen drawer, and so forth. The story was all very clever and amusing and would have been quite entertaining—but at my friend's expense. I thought, "What if she walked into church just before the sermon and sat down on the front row? Would I still be comfortable saying those things about her? When she came to church next week, would I want people saying, 'Oh, you're the anal-retentive friend whose visit the pastor was dreading! Nice to meet you!'"

Family members are an especially delicate area. My husband has asked me to refrain from using the story in any more sermons of how he installed a door camera on the front porch of our home. If someone rings the doorbell, the phone upstairs in his home office rings three times. If he turns the TV to channel 17, he can see who's on the front porch and decide whether to answer it or not. It saves him lots of trips up and down the stairs. This makes a great opening for a sermon on the friend at midnight in Luke 13. It's a good lead-in to a discussion of how we choose to whom to respond and to whom not to respond.

My husband is a good sport, but he eventually became annoyed by my telling and retelling of this story. I used it as the intro to an ordination sermon

I preached in Kansas, and it ended up on the Annual Conference Web site. After that, when people from other states met him they would say, "Oh, you're the guy with the door camera." I guess I see his point. It does kind of connect him with the guy who won't get out of bed to help a friend in need. But it's so tempting to ask for forgiveness rather than permission if a story is really good. Still, I've learned to reverse the sequence and always ask permission first. That way, I can say, "My husband So-and-so has given me permission to share this story." And he did.

Don't tell stories in which you're always the hero or heroine. Not too many preachers do this, but some do. "The car was on fire. Twenty cars were stopped around it just watching it burn. I knew that being a Good Samaritan was what our faith calls us to, despite the risks. I approached the car and pried open the door. I then pulled the unconscious woman out. By then, a number of other people had gathered around to help. Sometimes one leader is all it takes." So the preacher did something heroic. That's good. How do you talk about it without sounding like a superhero or heroine in tights and a cape? Maybe acknowledge the internal doubts and obstacles that attend such an act: "I hesitated, fear filling my mind. What if I got sued? What if I got hurt?" A preacher with this hero complex will often identify with Jesus or God in a story: "I always offer hospitality to the people on the outskirts. They are the Zacchaeus in the tree of life." "I always run to meet those who have hurt me and have returned, but it takes such faith . . ." (Prodigal Son)

An antidote to this tendency is to identify intentionally with the person behaving badly in a text. Then we come up with more convicting questions: "Does our exclusion ever hamper anyone from seeing Jesus?" "Does our mistreatment of others in the past ever make us dread the sight of them?" (Jacob and Esau in Gen. 32). "We'd prefer to see ourselves, like Bartimaeus, throwing off the cloak of our security and going boldly forward to meet Jesus, but aren't we more likely to fold the cloak and put it over our arm and creep along slowly to meet Jesus? It's good to have a fallback plan if Jesus can't do anything for our condition."

Keep in mind that this kind of hero complex can find its way subtly into sermons. You don't have to tell stories about rescuing people from burning cars to throw in little "Look how great I am" comments. Pastor John is preaching a sermon that ostensibly is about the importance of the church in our lives and our need to encourage people to worship with us. Here is his story: "I ran into a woman at Walgreens this week. I recognized her as a frequent visitor I hadn't seen for a while and greeted her warmly as I do everyone I meet when I'm out and about. 'I love your preaching!' she said. 'I've been caring for my mom and haven't been to church for a while, but I want to join now. I heard you'll be on vacation this next month, so I'm going to wait till you're back in the pulpit to start coming again.' I told her firmly, 'No waiting! You need to come home now! It's always the right time to come to church.'"

This story doesn't have the drama of a burning car, but it's clear that this preacher wants to be admired for his extroverted ways and wants everyone to know that people prefer his preaching to anyone else's on the staff.

Don't tell stories in which you always appear like a hapless buffoon. It can be effective to tell the occasional story of your saying the wrong thing to your daughter and making her cry or having to go to traffic school for rolling through a stop sign on your way home from church. But don't feed your people a steady diet of what a goofball you are. Listeners get tired of this as quickly as they do stories that involve picturing you in a cape and tights. They need for us to portray ourselves accurately, as fellow pilgrims, but also as trail guides. So share the progress you have made in the faith. Share the way you handled a situation differently a week ago from how you would have handled it a year ago. Share your joy in the faith.

Don't tell stories that involve listeners picturing you naked. We paint pictures with our words and stories, so be careful what pictures you paint. So you received an insight into the cleansing power of God's love in the shower on the mission trip as the cleansing and healing water cascaded over your body. Find another setting to tell about your epiphany.

Nakedness can also be seen metaphorically. There is a difference between appropriate self-revelation that says "I'm real," and publicly exposing yourself. Listeners will have the same three-part response to your inappropriate pulpit self-exposure as they would to the misguided individual in the public park in the gaping trench coat:

1. Eeewww!
2. This is weird.
3. Why is he or she doing this?

I don't think anyone needs details of my two labors and deliveries and my miscarriage. People don't need details of the preacher's private life with his or her spouse. If the preacher ever got drunk in college, the congregation would not need to know details of that particular event.

If the preacher has come back from addiction, a crisis of faith, or a deep depression following a bereavement, that is another matter. Then the point of sharing is the redemptive journey. That is a testimonial sermon, and even then we don't need all the physical details of the detox. We have reality TV for that. But a testimonial is different from the sharing of random negative tidbits about yourself that serve no purpose but to expose you at a level that is not appropriate in a sermon and that undermines your pastoral credibility.

I understand the concept of being transparent, but let's go for opaque. Think of it this way: Would you wear transparent clothes to preach in? Just because you thought it, or it happened to you, or you did it does not mean you have to share it. We call once again on the principle of "preach out of your own experience, but not always explicitly about it."

Don't tell stories that are not true. I know a pastor who has invented a fictional character, Old Jim. He tells stories about Old Jim. He has sermons that are basically short stories in which Old Jim is a key character. It's a Garrison Keillor–type move. It works because everyone knows Old Jim is a fictional character, the invention of their somewhat eccentric but creative pastor. It also works because he doesn't bring Old Jim out too often. If you're going to make up a creative story, signal listeners that that is what it is. "Imagine if . . . ," or "Here is a story that never happened but that always does," or the time-honored "Once upon a time . . ."

The basic advice here is don't tell stories as if they were true if they are not. You can tinker with the details of a story. I tell a story about a stained-glass window in the church of my childhood. It had three panes. In my story, I give it two, because I'm making a theological point about Jesus' humanity and divinity. If changing a detail doesn't hurt, mislead, or misrepresent anyone and makes your point clearer, feel free to do so. But don't tell someone else's story as if it happened to you. And don't make up a story and present it as a real event.

Don't Tell Stories the Wrong Way

Don't overhype your stories before you tell them. Don't introduce your story with a comment like "I'm about to tell you an incredibly moving story" or "I'm about to tell you the funniest joke I've heard in years." Let listeners be the judge of how moving or amusing a story is.

Don't explain your reason for telling the story after you have told it: "I've told you this story because it makes the point of the sermon that . . ." or "This little story, though amusing on the surface, carries the deeper lesson that . . ."

If the story fits the theme of the sermon, the reason you have told it should go without saying. Be especially careful not to go into explanation mode after an opening story as you are moving to the text. The fit between the two needs to be so tight that you don't need to say things like these: "You may wonder how this opening story relates to our text" or "This joke about someone jumping out of an airplane thinking he's holding a parachute pack but actually holding a knapsack is analogous to our text for this morning in which our Lord talks of how it is possible to gain the world and lose one's soul. Grasping the knapsack of the world rather than the parachute of the good news is the way we lose our souls even though we may think gathering an impressive collection of material possessions is the path to the good life." This kind of explanatory segue is both unnecessary and annoying to listeners, because they've already figured it out for themselves.

Don't tell us about the story; invite us into the story. A common piece of advice that veteran novelists give novices is "Show, don't tell." Think zoom lens. Think all five senses. Think setting. It bears repeating that every story has characters, a plot, a setting, and a theme. So invite us into the story rather than leaving us standing on the porch, peering through the window.

Put a spatial and temporal frame around your story. We tend to tell a lot of generalized stories without much of a context. Every story has a setting. Paint a frame around your story so we know where and when we are.

Here is a brief scene:

A pinkish sunset glows in the sky behind the gleaming silver diner. You pull into the driveway behind it, tires scrunching on gravel. As soon as you open the door, the smell of baking pies hits you.

Here is a generalized, sceneless telling of a story:

She and her husband had been in conflict for some months over the loss of his job and her resentment at the drop in the family budget. Arguments and harsh words often filled the air. It had gotten so bad this last time that she knew something had to change. He had left for a few days, and she was trying to figure things out.

When we tell a story, we leave people on the edges of it, giving them information about it. When we show people a story, we tie ideas to sensory details. These details invite listeners into the story to experience it with their senses. Showing people a story involves inviting them into a specific scene rather than telling them a generalized account of events. Sometimes that may mean starting in the middle of a scene (often called *in media res*, Latin for "in the middle of things") and filling in details later.

She sat at her kitchen table, after the door slammed shut after him, just staring at the pair of glasses on the table. Were they his or hers? Glasses made things clearer usually. She picked up the glasses and turned them over and over in her hands. With glasses you could see other people better. You could see yourself better when you looked in a mirror. Were those words he'd hissed at her true? Was she more in love with money than him?

Were his words true? That she was so focused on how his being fired had affected her that she didn't care how it had hurt him? Had she been wearing selfish glasses?

What to Say in Stories

Tell your own story. Have a testimonial story in your sermon barrel. Be able and ready to tell your own story. All preachers should have a testimonial sermon that tells the story of how they came to faith and how they are grow-ing in the faith. This takes the form of an extended story that is grounded in Scripture. The preacher is the illustration of the sermon. But don't preach this one every week.

Tell stories from the nonfiction best-seller you are reading. Several books have caught my eye lately. They are on a stack on my nightstand: *The Lucifer Effect* by Philip Zimbardo, *Dish: How Gossip Became the News and the New Became Just Another Show* by Jeannette Walls, *Loneliness: Human Nature and the Need for Social Connection* by John T. Cacippo and William Patrick, and *What the Dog Saw and Other Adventures* by Malcolm Gladwell.

Tell stories from the novel you are reading. I read light fiction as an escape, but I rarely find sermon fodder there. Not so in novels such as *The Poison-wood Bible* by Barbara Kingsolver, *The Glass Castle* by Jeannette Walls, *Gilead* by Marilynne Robinson, *March* by Geraldine Brooks, *Empire Falls* by Richard Russo, and *The Brief Wondrous Life of Oscar Wao* by Junot Díaz. Use the principles of scene and sensory detail I've already discussed. Pull out a brief vignette that makes your point. Only include the details that are abso-lutely necessary for people who have not read the book to be able to connect with the story. Don't be like the person who has the gift of being able to tell you the plot of an hour-and-a-half-long movie in just 100 minutes.

Use an example from a movie. Be brief, and make sure someone who hasn't seen the movie will be moved by the story. Film clips can be effective as long as they are brief and well presented, without time lags and technology glitches.

Tell stories from history. It's not a good idea to always tell Mother Teresa stories, stories of larger-than-life people who made sacrifices we are unlikely to make. These stories are too easy to dodge, because we know we could never come up to snuff. Do tell stories from Christian history: St. Francis and his call to service, Catherine Booth and her inner struggle in accepting the call to preach, John Wesley and his warmed heart, or Phoebe Palmer and her faith that would not die even in the midst of the loss of her children.

Tell stories from other traditions. Tell rabbinic stories. Tell stories, legends, and fables from other cultures. Tell about how Buddha began life as a rich prince and for many years did not know of the suffering in the world. Tell stories that help people understand and appreciate other faiths.

Tell stories that get at how the Good News would sound to people who are not present in worship. Tell the story of one prisoner sharing a psalm with another. Share the story of a survivor of the earthquake in Haiti doubting God or affirming her faith in God. Be on the lookout for stories that show us how someone who is not here and is not from a background like ours hears and lives the Good News. How does my message that God cares for our needs sound to a person who has lost her home in an earthquake? How does the message some preachers preach of prosperity to those who have faith sound to a child with poor parents? How does the message that God raises up the poor and puts down the mighty sound to a homeless teenager? Why not articulate such questions as we preach? They may be questions no one is asking but that we all need to ask, preachers as well as people. Find stories from unlikely people in overlooked places in your community to convict and motivate your congregation.

Tell stories from the perspective of nameless people in texts and in our contemporary contexts. Look for the people in the biblical text who are not named and ask, "What is their story? What would the Good News look like to them?"

Tell stories through the lenses of images and metaphors. In his book *Surviving the Sermon*, David Schlafer points out that there are three factors that unify a sermon: story, image, and theme. Depending on the sermon, one or the other may be in the driver's seat, but all three need to be present (Schlafer 1992, 66). What we have said about stories is also true for images. They need to connect with listeners but not trivialize the sermon. We need to employ images in our sermons for the same reasons we employ stories: because they are biblical and incarnational and because they speak to the depths of people's lives, to their self-conceptions and motivations.

In her book *Imagery for Preaching*, Patricia Wilson Kastner reminds us that imagery is not just visual. It represents the whole sensory world of the text and our context. That includes all we can see, touch, hear, smell, and taste. Such an expanded view of imagery calls for heightened attentiveness to two worlds: ours and that of the text. Ignatian meditation, in which we enter imaginatively into the physical world of the text, is an invaluable resource in preparing to preach. An image that we single out and use to bear some of the thematic weight of the sermon becomes a metaphor.

How do I decide on a metaphor for a sermon? Ask the text two questions: First, what images does it offer to describe our human condition? Second, what images does it offer to describe the character of God and how God relates to our condition? Putting those two in conversation can often lead to a dynamic, vivid sermon. Here are some examples: fishing all night without a catch and nets overflowing with fish; a deer longing for flowing streams and stream of living water; wandering in the wilderness and walking in joyful procession to the house of God.

Keep in mind that any sensory feature of the text can become a metaphor. This extends to actions. So Abram taking the first step of his journey can become a metaphor for our walk with God. The breaking of the alabaster jar is a metaphor for our pouring ourselves out in service to God and others. Ruth gleans in the fields, Isaiah cowers in the temple while the seraph wings its way toward him with a burning coal to place on his lips, God kneels in the dirt and fashions a human being, a city gleams in the distance where there will be no more tears, and Paul tries to pull the thorn out of his flesh. Metaphors. The fields are ripe for our harvest.

Rather than bypassing the rich metaphors of the text, feast upon them. In his book *Design for Preaching*, H. Grady Davis wonders why preachers go beyond the lush foliage of the sermon to import illustrations that are not congruous with the imagery of the text. He says it reminds him of a tree with brightly colored kites caught in its branches. The lush branches of most textual trees contain enough metaphorical fruit for our sermons without our importing illustrations from other metaphorical mind-sets. If the text is full of boats, fish, and water, stick with examples that have that same imagery set. Find contemporary analogies instead of shifting the metaphor and importing examples that deal with car engines, or making meatloaf, or sports.

Clearly, stories are a rich, fruitful resource for preaching, which itself partakes of an overarching saving story.

Questions for Reflection

1. Why am I telling this story?
2. Is it another story about me in a long line of stories about me?
3. Is it a substitute for substance?
4. Am I bored with the text and trying to compensate?
5. Does the story work against the theme of my sermon?
6. Does it trivialize God or how we are to respond to God?

7. If it is humorous, does it inspire smiles and laughter for a reason in keeping with my sermon's theme?
8. Does the story have a different agenda from the text?
9. Does it denigrate a particular person or group?
10. Do I have permission to tell it?
11. Am I the hero or heroine, in either obvious or subtle ways?
12. Does the story represent appropriate self-revelation or public exposure of one's private parts?
13. Is the story true?
14. If I am presenting a fictionalized story, have I signaled listeners to this effect?
15. Have I overhyped the story before I tell it or overexplained it after I've told it?
16. Have I invited people into the story or just told them about it?
17. Have I put a frame around the story: presenting it as a scene with a particular setting that listeners can see, hear, taste, smell, and touch?

Chapter 8

What Not to Say (and What to Say) at the End

Definition of an optimist: a woman in the choir who puts her shoes back on the first time the preacher says, "And in conclusion . . ."

I once heard a preacher say, "Ending a sermon well is like trying to get out of a canoe gracefully."

*T*wo analogies come to mind when I think about ending a sermon. The first is the breakup of a romantic relationship. The second is leaving a party. In both cases, it is not always hard to end things, but it is often hard to end things well.

There are at least three lame ways to end a relationship: the texted breakup, the Facebook breakup, and the back-and-forth breakup. The first is the Texted Breakup. When applied to a sermon, the texted breakup has the preacher reading an uninspiring summation of the main points of the sermon. A summary ending can be effective, but not if it's boring and if it is read rather than delivered. When we end a sermon with our congregation, let's at least have the decency to look them in the eye.

Secondly, we have the Facebook Breakup. In a Facebook breakup, without prior notice, one party changes his or her relationship status and removes pictures. When applied to a sermon, this is the ending that is like galloping toward a cliff, with the William Tell Overture as the soundtrack, then coming to a screeching halt. It is clumsy and unanticipated.

Finally, we have the Back and Forth Breakup. "I'm not really into this, but I don't know how to get out of it." Applied to a sermon, the back-and-forth breakup becomes the multiple ending sermon. More on that later.

The second analogy that points up just how difficult ending things can be in a sermon is the analogy of leaving a party. If it's a large, lively party, you can slip away without being observed. But suppose it's a smaller, meal-focused party. Then leaving is trickier. Too early is rude. Too late is probably even worse.

My husband and I have friends who came to dinner last month. She is a nurse and often works an early morning shift. She is also a very straightforward person. As an aside, some of my best preaching students in the past have been former nurses. Their personalities and demeanors offer a good combination of comfort, competence, practicality, and honesty—not bad qualities for preachers.

But back to my story. After we had had dinner and had been sitting around talking for an hour, she looked at her husband and said, "We need to go now. I have to get up at 5:30 in the morning. Then she looked at me, smiled, and said, "We have had a lovely time. Thank you for the fine food and company." And then they left.

No starting a new conversation at the door. No wandering around trying to gather up coat, purse, or casserole dish with crusty residue around the edges. No coming back for a forgotten umbrella. A clean, polite exit. I thought as she left, "You go, girl." And sure enough, she did.

For what it's worth, never go back for your umbrella. Keep on moving. It's too late to go back. It will be an awkward, anticlimactic moment that will annoy your host. It would be like standing back up after you've just said "Amen" and sat down, and then saying, "Wait, there is one more thing."

When it comes to sermons, it's more difficult to make an exit than an entrance. The first step to recovery from any bad habit is to acknowledge that we have it. So I say we acknowledge that it is no easy matter to end a sermon well and that our current methods are not always effective. Our next step will be to explore some of the ways it can go awry, followed by suggesting some more effective strategies.

Preachers and teachers of preaching like to talk about the preacher's toolbox. That is a positive metaphor. It signifies a repertoire of useful, effective sermonic strategies. There is also a preacher's trash bin, a receptacle where we ought to put all the ineffective sermon strategies we don't ever want to use again.

What Not to Say at the End

The Holy-Spirit-Rescue Ending

This is otherwise known as the "I'm just going to leave it all up to the Holy Spirit" ending. I have it on good authority that the Holy Spirit is available for consultation during our sermon preparation and not just during our sermon delivery. That means that the Holy Spirit could conceivably assist me in planning an effective ending for my sermon on Friday afternoon as well as assist me in offering it to the congregation on Sunday morning. It hardly seems fair to not consult someone and then blame them when we ramble around. Roman Catholic homiletician Ken Untener has good advice on this point: "Don't ever begin to preach a homily unless you know what your last two sentences are going to be. . . . Going into an ending unprepared is like going into a haunted house without a flashlight. The demons are lurking there ready to leap out: repetition, church-speak, filler, a new thought" (Untener 1999, 29).

Much of my advice about what not to say has to do with endings that go on and on and on. It's a rather rare problem to have a preacher who habitually ends sermons abruptly and without prior notice. But it can happen. And when it does, it reminds me of the story a friend of mine who is an airline pilot told me recently. A pilot who had just made captain was serving with him on a domestic flight. The newly appointed captain had not landed well. The plane had hit the ground with a decided bump rather than a smooth glide. It had landed so hard, in fact, that the oxygen masks had all come down, a phenomenon the flight attendants call "the orange grove." There was a rap on the cockpit door. The pilot opened it an inch. There stood a flight attendant with a bright smile on her face. "Captain, I just was wondering: did we land, or were we shot down?"

The Cruel-Tease Ending

The more common problem with endings is continuing to fly the plane when we should have landed it and sat down. This is the false ending. It would be as if an airline pilot came on the loudspeaker and announced that he had begun the descent to the airport, told everyone to get in their seats and fasten their seatbelts and the flight attendants to prepare for landing, and then lifted the plane's nose again and kept on circling the airport. It is also known as the interstate highway ending. The interstate highway ending is the ending in which the preacher passes several perfectly good exits but stays on the highway. The whole purpose of preaching is to give people hope, but genuine hope in Christ, not the false hope that the sermon's ending is going to come before our Lord's return. Untener quotes an anonymous layperson's comments on his priest's homily endings: "We know when he's done, but that doesn't mean he stops" (Untener 1999, 30). If the preacher circles the airport too many times, people grab their parachutes and exit the plane.

Picture all the passengers parachuting to the ground while the preacher-pilot, oblivious to their exit, is still in the cockpit, making announcements over the loudspeaker.

I once heard Madonna interviewed about relationships. And who better? She said, "Relationships are like chewing gum. When they start out they are juicy and full of flavor. But after a while, they become a gray, tasteless glob that you can't wait to spit out." To avoid such negative listener response to our sermons, don't send signals that you're ending when you're not ending. Avoid phrases like "In conclusion," or "And so in closing," which signal endings and annoy people if you then do not end. Worse yet are the little phrases that let people know we're aware that we're going on too long but just can't help ourselves. Things like "This final story will be brief, I promise," or "Bear with me while I share with you one more point," or "And finally—yes, folks, I'm really not going to keep you here till suppertime. Ha ha ha!" Going on too long is no laughing matter. Trying to make a joke of one's verbosity is only going to heighten the irritation factor.

The Nuclear Fission Ending

Whereas the cruel-tease ending announces an ending and doesn't really end, the nuclear fission ending begins a whole new line of thought right at the end (Untener 1999, 31). And then another and then another. It's like being on a plane whose pilot repeatedly touches down on the runway, then guns the engine and takes off again, each time toward a whole new destination. Or maybe it's like pulling up to the gate, only to realize that you're in a remote location from which you must deplane to board a bus, and then a train, and then a shuttle, all part of a seemingly interminable journey toward the terminal. (That's enough airplane metaphors for the nuclear fission ending. I think I just split a couple of atoms myself.)

Ken Unterer's advice here is excellent: "Do not verbalize the new thought that comes into your mind toward the end of your sermon. Stick with the plan. Ad-libbed endings don't fuel an ending. They make it fizzle" (Untener 1999, 30). When the preacher becomes an Energizer bunny just when everyone's heard as much as they can handle, the only one energized is the preacher.

I strongly suspect that our sermons drive people to pray while they are listening. As the preacher arrives at a perfectly good stopping point, people say to themselves, "Dear God, let her say 'Amen' and sit down!"

The old advice for public speakers isn't half bad: "Stand up. Speak up. Shut up" (Becker 1973, 52). The end of a sermon is a time to reinforce, underscore, or place an exclamation point on teaching that has already been offered. It is not the time for the preacher to pull up in a front loader and dump a whole load of biblical and theological elaboration onto the congregation. Novelists call this "clumping"—dumping too much description into the flow that interrupts the action and causes people to stop reading and start watching TV. The end of the sermon is not the time that the congregation can absorb nuances and qualifiers and conceptual elaborations. The time for new teaching is not the end, when listener fatigue is likely to have set in.

The Backing-Over-the-Spikes Ending

I've rented enough cars in my travels to have seen the same sign many times. You drive into the rental car return gate and it is the first thing you see in bold black letters: "Don't back over the spikes." I always have the impulse to try it and see what would really happen, but I don't. Because I know. The tires would deflate. Deflation is the effect of the backing-over-the-spikes sermon ending too. Any hope, joy, or motivation the sermon has stirred in listeners deflates. Why? Because in the backing-over-the-spikes ending, the preacher puts the sermon in reverse. The preacher has enumerated the temptations we face in daily life, then, near the end, has presented the Good News that God offers us a safe haven from temptation in practices of devotion. Then the preacher reverts to a repeated enumeration of the challenges to these practices.

Or the preacher defines the obligations of discipleship at home, in the community, and in the workplace, then, near the end, affirms that it is Jesus Christ who empowers us to discipleship in all these spheres, that it is through his presence and power that we can live faithfully. The preacher then reverts to "you must," "you ought," and "you should." Any kind of encouragement to action at the end of a sermon needs to use "you can" or "we can" language. Don't revert to "you should" when it is time for "you can."

The Debbie Downer Ending

Debbie Downer is a character in skits on *Saturday Night Live* who introduces morbid, depressing topics at birthdays parties and other festive occasions. She throws a wet blanket on any ember of hope in a particular situation. If you're about to take a bite of your birthday cake, she'll tell you how much cholesterol is in the frosting and offer statistics on the rate at which glucose levels rise on the ingestion of processed carbohydrates and simple sugars. If you've just adopted a cat from the local shelter, she'll tell you how many cats are being put to death around the world at that very moment, despite your paltry effort.

The Debbie Downer ending, a variation of the backing-over the-spikes ending, is one that revisits the pain and grimness of the human condition after having pointed listeners to places where God is at work bringing grace and hope in the world. It says, "God's Grace is wonderful, but it's not enough because there is still sin in the world." I don't need to go into all the reasons that this is bad theology.

A preacher using the backing-over-the-spikes ending or the Debbie Downer ending would be like a pilot who is supposed to fly his plane from Dallas to Denver but who turns the plane around near the Denver airport so that when everyone gets off the plane, they're back in Dallas.

The Deflating Balloon Ending

This is the ending in which the preacher tells a story that summarizes her sermon at the end, pauses dramatically, raising the false hope that the sermon is over, and then launches into explanation mode. If you need to summarize your sermon, do it before that moving final story. It's easier to move from explanation to emotion than from emotion to explanation.

The Ice-Cream Sundae Ending

When I lived in Pennsylvania, I used to eat at a Friendly's restaurant, where the motto was "Great ice cream, too," but actually the ice cream was more of a draw than the fried clam sandwiches with coleslaw or the Friendlyburger with fries. Friendly's offered meal deals that were capped off with an ice-cream sundae, a single scoop of ice cream with the sauce of your choice—chocolate, marshmallow, peanut butter, strawberry, or butterscotch—whipped cream, a cherry, and crushed peanuts. A sermon with an ice-cream sundae ending concludes with a happy story or a reassuring statement that doesn't ring true for listeners. There could be a number of reasons for this response. Maybe the sermon oversimplifies a complex issue. Maybe it offers what feels like a false promise that everything will work out if we just have enough faith or think the right thoughts. Maybe the sermon has vividly illustrated the negative (e.g., examples of child abuse) and then tried to rely on conceptual language to convey the Good News: "Despite these examples of horror, God is still at work in our world."

This is also known as the stick-on bow ending. We all know that stick-on bows don't always stick.

The Honey-Do Ending

This ending says, "Here is the one thing you must do this week if you are really a Christian or if you are genuine in your response to this message." All that has gone before in the sermon boils down to this one thing: go downstairs and adopt a child for a small monthly fee.

I can see during Lent, suggesting a particular discipline of biblical mediation and having it outlined in the bulletin. I can see suggesting areas of service in the community as options for faithful response. But the "to-do" list as a weekly staple of sermon endings becomes predictable and prescriptive and thereby lose its force. What if another response had come to someone's mind earlier in the sermon? Does the preacher's prescription always trump the listener's inspiration?

This leads to a final, more general piece of advice on what not to say at the end: Don't end a sermon the same way every time.

What to Say at the End

The Symmetrical Ending

Story Symmetry

With this strategy, the preacher ends the sermon by completing the story with which he began the sermon. For example, the sermon begins with Wayne sitting by the lake reflecting on his life and the fears that are churning inside him. It leaves him sitting there and goes on to explore fear and faith in the book of Proverbs. Finally, the preacher says, "We left Wayne sitting by the lake," and then goes into Wayne's experience of recognizing God's peace as he gazes over the lake. This is a nice symmetrical move, with two provisos: (1) you can't use it every week, and (2) you can't leave Wayne sitting by the lake.

In a sermon, I once left two teenage boys, Will and John, fighting their way through a blizzard in the Arctic wilderness after their plane crashed and the pilot died. I forgot to finish the story at the end and had to work the news of their rescue into the benediction. It's pretty hard to pretend you did such a thing on purpose.

Image Symmetry

Similar to the story-symmetry ending, here the sermon ends with the image with which it began. Texts teem with images, sensory cues to the world of the text. The Bible pulses with trees planted by streams of water, cities set on hills, lamps under bushel baskets, bubbling pools that cannot heal, living water that can, and so on. Be alert to the whole sensory world of the text and your context.

I once preached a sermon that used the metaphor of a parachute jump to illustrate Jesus' proverb "Those who want to save their life will lose it, and those who lose their life for my sake, and the sake of the Gospel, will save it." Trying to save your life is the freefall, Jesus' saying is the rip cord, and the parachute opening is the experience of finding our lives when we lose them. My goal was that this metaphor would provide a memorable opening and closing for the sermon as well as give it thematic unity. Often an image seeks a larger role than we have given it. An image that may have come to you well into your preparation time may deserve to have a leading role in the sermon.

The "So Now What?" Ending

This is the positive version of the honey-do ending. It offers moral guidance toward faithful responses to the Gospel. It could take the form of a story that shows people living in that way or an imagined scenario that answers the question "What if we lived by the Gospel as presented in sermon? What would our lives look like?" In both cases, the story and the "What if?" scenario, the goal is to open up or suggest options for faithful action, not to narrow the sermon down to a bulleted chore list or a commercial for involvement in a particular cause.

The "So now what?" ending could take the form of a story that shows people living out the response to the message, embodying the positive theme of the sermon. Maybe you are preaching on Matthew 8:18–27 and end with a story of someone learning faith in the high gales of life. Maybe you're preaching a sermon called "Finders Weepers, Losers Keepers" on Jesus' aforementioned proverb. You end with a story of a group of youth experiencing joy in losing their vision of life as self-gratification and gaining an experience of God's presence in serving the poor.

To make this kind of ending effective, you need to do two things:

1. Step aside and allow the characters in the story to end the sermon through their actions and dialogue.

2. Present the story as a slice of life, as an example of faithful response, not the definition of faithful response. So if my story is of a couple that adopted a Down's syndrome child, I don't leave people with the impression that if they have not adopted a special needs child or don't plan to, they are not true disciples of Jesus Christ.

A "So now what?" ending could paint a scenario of what the church, our community, or our individual lives would look like if we lived by the Good News. Whatever form it takes, its purpose is to inspire and to direct listeners to active response.

Here is an example of a "So now what?" ending from a sermon preached by Nora Tubbs Tisdale called "God's No and Ours," based on Galatians 5:1 and Esther 1:1–22. Tisdale's theme is the call for the church to support those who are being abused and participate in their freedom from bondage. She uses the story of Queen Vashti's refusal to appear at King Ahasuerus's banquet, coupled with Galatians' words on freedom from bondage, as the scriptural basis for her sermon. Here is her conclusion: "For freedom God in Christ has set all of us free. Therefore, let us stand firm—not only for our own sakes, but also with and on behalf of others in the church who desperately need us to stand firm with them—and let us boldly and courageously open our mouths and say NO! to anything and everything that would require any of God's children to submit again to a yoke of slavery" (Tisdale 1998, 206).

The Celebration Ending

The celebration ending is a gift of African American preaching to the whole church. It is characterized by eloquent, poetic language, the use of refrains that have punctuated the sermon, and a joyful intensity of emotion in affirming our saving faith. Often words to familiar songs or hymns are quoted, as well as inspiring scriptural quotations.

Here are three pieces of advice regarding the celebration ending: First, if you are going to end the sermon on an eloquent, emotionally celebratory tone, be aware that you need to build up to it. The advice of skilled African American preachers for years has been "Start slow, go higher, strike fire." Their advice is superb and should not be ignored. If you start high, where do you have to go from there?

The second piece of advice is practice, practice, practice. Here is an excerpt from the ending of a sermon by Gardner Taylor called "In His Own Clothes," based on Mark 15:20. You can see the qualities of eloquent language, poignant imagery, and use of refrain that contribute to the power of this kind of ending, which is often called an "affective ending." You can also see how important it is for the preacher to know the ending well so that it can be delivered with the confidence and passion it deserves.

> In his own clothes he went to Calvary and made everything right, not temporarily all right but for always. . . . Once for all. It is all right now. The crooked way has been made straight; we may arise and shine, for our light is come. It is all right now.

> We shall see him yet in other clothes . . . on that day when Christ shall appear with an old, faded red cloak around his shoulders, no longer mocked by soldiers, no longer wearing simple garments of this earth. Every eye shall see him. We will see him as heaven's king, victor over death, hell and the grave, the admired of angels. Every eye shall see him. Ten thousand times ten thousand and thousands and thousands of angels and the triumphant sons and daughters of God will escort him. His raiment will outshine the sun. And on his vesture, his garment, a name will be written, "King of King and Lord of Lords." Shall we not shout his name who has lifted us to heights sublime and made us his own people forever? (Taylor 1994, 291–92)

The final piece of advice in preaching a celebratory ending is to preach it in a way that fits the occasion, the text, and your personality and preaching style. The emotions involved in celebration can vary in intensity. Fireworks are good, but so is a glowing candle. A shouted "Hallelujah!" is wonderful, but a whisper can command attention too. Change it up, and keep them wondering. Anticipation is the key dynamic in gaining and maintaining listener attention, both in individual sermons and from week to week.

The Summation Ending

In both the celebration ending and the summation ending, it's important to use language reminiscent of the opening that carries through the body of the sermon.

While we don't want to end every sermon with a summary of the teaching of the sermon, sometimes this can be very effective. I once preached a sermon called "Now Appearing" on 1 Corinthians 15:1–11 ("Last of all, as to one untimely born, he appeared also to me"). The theme of the sermon was that the resurrection was not just good news for people of the past, but for people facing all sorts of issues in the present. The sermon unfolded with examples of people in various conditions—depression, illness, facing difficult decisions—who showed how the power of the living Christ spoke to their situation. Since the stories had already contained a lot of emotional freight, I decided on a summation ending that employed a refrain that had appeared throughout the sermon: "Jesus is now appearing."

"Jesus is now appearing to the depressed," I said. "Jesus is now appearing to those suffering from various diseases." Jesus is now appearing to those who think life has passed them by.

The summary ending succeeds if it follows the advice of the Vermont proverb "Talk less, say more." You've already said it, now just restate key phrases and sit down. I sometimes think of this as the bouquet ending. You pull several stems out of the sermon garden and, at the end, bind them in a bouquet and hand them to the congregation to take home. The summation ending is not a lengthy presentation of new teachings.

In a sermon on Mark 8:34–37 called "Finders Weepers, Losers Keepers," I touched on the way a number of people in Mark's Gospel, in trying to save their lives, actually lost them. The ending reflects this earlier theme:

> They say sometimes to get people's attention, you have to whisper. Into the din, the noise of Pharisees wrangling about whose hands were the cleanest, a boy banging his head on rocks, unable to shake his demon by himself, disciples arguing over who would get the best seats in the kingdom, and a rich man wailing at the thought of giving up his possessions—into all this noise Jesus speaks. He speaks one short, not-so-sweet little saying. It sums up his life and his teachings. Living by it is why he died. And his presence with us is how we can live by it until we die, to live unto eternal life. (McKenzie 2008)

In a sermon called "Nobody Else," I dealt with the rejection of Jesus at Nazareth in Luke 4:14–30. I also wove the idea from Luke 2:40 about the child growing and becoming strong into the sermon as a way to express how Jesus' influence in our lives can grow with time.

> The text ends in this mysterious and hopeful way: "Jesus, passing through the midst of them, went on his way."
>
> You can't get rid of him so easily.
>
> He wants to grow and become strong in your life so that it's no secret to you or others that anxiety is weakening and peace is growing, that condemnation is weakening and forgiveness is growing, that apathy toward the suffering of others is weakening and passion for justice is growing.
>
> And the child grew and became strong.
>
> Filled with wisdom and the favor of God was upon him.
>
> May it be so in you and in our church this Epiphany season. (McKenzie 2007a)

The summation ending sums up key thoughts so that a concept stays in listeners' minds. One option here is to end with a line from the Scripture lesson that is particularly inspiring and makes the key point of the sermon. A good example would be "Do not worry about anything, but in everything by prayer and supplication with thanksgiving let your requests be made known to God. And the peace of God that surpasses all understanding will guard your hearts and your minds in Christ Jesus" (Phil. 4:6–7).

The Story Ending

The story ending embodies the sermon's focus and function (theme and purpose). If my sermon is designed to inspire people to trust God, I might end with a story of someone who moved from fear to faith. Maybe I tell the story of my friend Iva, who was afraid to preach. After weeks of visualizing Jesus standing with his arm around her, a six-year-old girl came up and showed her a picture she had drawn in her children's bulletin of Jesus in the front of the church while Pastor Iva preached.

If the sermon has more than one story, you need to put the most moving one at the end. Starting out with an emotionally moving story makes pretty much anything that comes after it seem anticlimactic. To maximize the impact of an inspiring closing story, don't precede it with stories that are too emotionally taxing. A series of stories, all at a high emotional level (sad, poignant, painful, etc.), leaves people feeling wrung out, even manipulated. You don't want listeners to be emotionally drained to the point where they miss out on your closing story. Think about what happens to elastic when it gets overstretched. It makes that crinkly sound and doesn't return to its original shape.

Closing stories can do other things besides warm the heart. William Willimon has a sermon called "What Time Is It?" in which his goal is to help us see the urgency of answering the call to discipleship. He tells of attending a funeral with his wife in which the preacher declared that while it was too late for the deceased, it was not too late for them to hear God's word and repent. On the drive home, Willimon was complaining that the sermon was manipulative and negative. His wife replied, "Of course, the worst part of all is that what he said was true" (Willimon 1994, 109).

There is a story ending that is not a warm, reassuring appeal to the emotions, but an appeal to the intellect and will. So closing stories can appeal to will, emotions, or logic or some combination of all three. You the preacher must decide what kind of story will best convey the theme of your sermon.

Steve Langhofer, a pastor in Overland Park, Kansas, preached a sermon entitled "Cleaning Up Your Mess," based on Jesus' cleansing of the temple in Matthew 21:12–17. It ends with a story about Steve's dad, who was called in to clean out a relative's home after her death. The last line of the sermon is this: "My dad said to me, 'Steve, you wouldn't believe the stuff I found in that house. I sure hope when I die there won't be anything in my house that will embarrass you boys' " (Langhofer 2008). So Steve's dad has the last word in Steve's sermon, and Steve sits down. Another kind of kick in the gut ending, with no explanation needed.

The Open-Ended Ending

Usually this kind of ending, which provokes listeners to apply the message to their own lives, is challenging and a little uncomfortable:

> "Well, here we stand with these rocks in our hands. They are just the right size for throwing. Who wants to go first?" (sermon on John 8:1–11)
> "What on earth would possess someone who had just been forgiven of a great debt to turn around and be so harsh in judging someone else?" (sermon on Matt. 18:23–34)

Here is the ending of a meditation I wrote a few years ago on the parable of the Prodigal Son:

> We are left, at the end of the parable, not sure whether the older brother will go into the banquet hall or not. Maybe the affront to his sense of fairness will overpower his yearning for the forgiveness and joy that lie within the banquet hall. Maybe he will go off to the barn and fork some hay to work off his frustrations, while the sound of the festivities annoys his ears. Or maybe his yearning for the love that lies within the banquet hall will overcome all else, and he will enter into the joy of a God who rejoices over the return of every lost child. (McKenzie 2007b, 9)

An effective end strategy is to draw listeners into a scene, either biblical or contemporary, and leave them wondering how they would respond to the situation. The sermon needs to have equipped them to respond before this final scene. Often this takes the form of asking them what they would have said or done, in effect inviting them to identify with the character in the story or text, informed by the teaching of the sermon's beginning and middle.

I once ended a sermon on John 5, the man at the pool of Bethzatha, with a story from my first parish of a young man who had been out drinking and on the way home had hit a tree. After the accident, his friend, who had been in the passenger's seat, lay in ICU while he sat in my family room with his head in his hands. He looked up, his face ashen except for the red gash on his temple. "Jesus Christ, what am I going to do?" he asked.

I wasn't sure if it was a curse or a prayer.

How would you have answered him?

"And Jesus, seeing that he had been lying there a long time, asked him, 'Do you want to be healed?' How would you answer Jesus' question as you lie next to your pool?" (John 5)

The Ending of the Sermon Should Grow Out of the Beginning and the Middle

C. W. Smith, distinguished professor of English at Southern Methodist University and author of eight novels and numerous short stories, once spoke to my preaching class about what preachers can learn from novelists. Some fifteen seminary students sat in a circle and asked Smith questions about his craft that they could apply to their sermons. One student asked, "Do you have any advice for how to end a sermon?" Smith thought for a moment and said, "When I'm having trouble with an ending, it's because there is something off about the beginning and the middle. The ending should grow out of the beginning and the middle."

That sounds incredibly obvious, doesn't it? Yet if we think about it, that's what's wrong with most of the "What Not to Say" endings I mentioned earlier.

The Holy-Spirit-rescue ending doesn't grow out of what came before, because it is not planned. The cruel-tease ending drags out the sermon so that what came before is lost in our irritation with the fact that the sermon cannot seem to come to any satisfying conclusion. It's like the scarf I knitted for my dad when I was ten years old. It started out at a normal scarf width and grew wider and longer the more I knit. Even a man who, like my dad, was six feet, four inches tall, can't pull off a six-foot-long, two-foot-wide scarf. That's too much scarf for one neck.

The nuclear fission ending does not grow out of the beginning and the middle. It takes off on a new tangent right at the end, like a marathon runner distracted by a butterfly ten yards from the finish line.

The ice-cream sundae ending doesn't grow out of the beginning and the middle. Its happy-go-lucky, false reassurances are stick-on bows. An ice-cream sundae ending cannot be the logical conclusion of a sermon that has done justice to the pain of the human condition. We need reassurance that God is with us in our pain, not that if we have faith, there will be no pain.

This kind of ending reminds me of the ending of the movie *Slumdog Millionaire*. I know everyone loved that movie, but I thought the ending was too facile. It asked me as a viewer to leap from slum and violence and tragedy to reunited lovers and good fortune in one smooth Bollywood dance move. I didn't buy it.

My mom, who is a fabulous cook, used to say, "Weak entrée, strong dessert." As a dessert lover, I respect that advice. But it doesn't work for sermons. If I haven't presented something of substance in the body of the sermon, a shot of syrup isn't going to save it.

C. W. Smith's advice is really good. If my ending doesn't work, it is because there is either a substance problem or a sequence problem. Substance problems exist with endings in which the preacher introduces new material that the sermon has not paved the way for. In other words, the ending doesn't grow out of the beginning and the middle. Such endings are like a bad mystery novel that brings in some second cousin twice removed who has been raised by wolves as the killer with absolutely no foreshadowing.

A number of endings discussed in this chapter are ineffective because of a sequence problem. They reverse the forward flow of the sermon to a satisfying conclusion. This would be like a movie that, at the end when it's time for the love scene or the unveiling of the killer or the reunion of the family or whatever, launches into a flashback. There comes a time when we know enough of the backstory and it's time for the preacher to connect the good news of the story to our story.

Ineffective endings are often problems of sequence. The Debbie Downer ending revisits human sin and brutality when it is time to move toward Divine Grace and Redemption. The backing-over-the-spikes ending revisits the "ought" or the obligation when it's time to move toward the "can," the divine power to fulfill the ought. The deflating balloon ending reverses the sequence from a story that touches emotion and evokes response to a lecture about the story that pulls the plug on our motivation.

The Ending Should Match the Theme and Purpose of the Sermon in Both Its Logic and Its Emotional Tone

In his textbook *The Witness of Preaching*, Thomas G. Long advises preachers to have a focus (theme statement), a function (statement of the impact I want my sermon to have on listeners), and form (communication plan for the sequence by which the sermon unfolds). For more on this, see chapters 4 and 5 of the second edition of Long's book.

The Ending of the Sermon Should Be in Keeping
with Its Theme and Purpose

John Wesley's general method of preaching was "to invite, to convince, to offer Christ, to build up, and to do this in some measure in every sermon" (Wesley 1830, 480-486). He defined the general purpose of preaching as to "offer them Christ." Within that overarching goal, though, sermons have specific purposes. Preachers must ask themselves what the most effective ending would be to achieve their specific purpose. The ending is your chance to bring home the theme and accomplish your purpose, so the clearer you are in what your theme and purpose are, the clearer you can be in choosing your ending. There needs to be both a logical match and an emotive match. The ending can't make a point different from the sermon's theme. The emotional tone needs to grow out of the beginning and the middle of the sermon.

Here are two examples of a logical mismatch between sermon theme and ending: Suppose my goal is to reassure people that Christ is with them in suffering. I probably won't choose to end my sermon with a challenging question about their faith. Suppose my purpose is to challenge people's habit of valuing each other based on degree of worldly success. I probably won't end with a comforting story about Christ's presence in suffering.

If it's Lent and I'm trying to get people to reflect on their sins and repent, a humorous ending that makes light of our foibles would not be a match in terms of emotional tone. If there have been a number of deaths lately in the congregation and I'm trying to point people toward the stability of God in the ups and downs of life, I need for the ending to have stability and joy as its emotional tone. I probably would not opt for an open-ended sermon. My goal is to reassure, not cause people to question the depth of their faith in God.

The Ending of the Sermon Should Be the Logical Conclusion of Its Form

All the forces of the sermon should come together at the end: the logical theme, the purpose, and the form. The form of the sermon is the communication plan for the message. It indicates the sequence by which the preacher allows the sermon's themes, teaching, images, and stories to unfold. Many books outline the options for form for sermons. Eugene Lowry's form has come to be called "the Lowry Loop." David Buttrick talks in terms of the sermon as a series of "moves." Mike Graves advocates letting the sermon unfold as a "Homiletical Slide Show." Fred Craddock pioneered what has come to be called the "Inductive Sermon" form. Paul Scott Wilson has outlined a sermon form called "The Four Pages of the Sermon" in his book by the same name. Henry Mitchell pays tribute to the classic African American sermon form that takes the shape of "Celebration."

Those who advocate having the sermon take the form of the text believe that texts, like sermons, don't just want to say things but to do things. So the ending would be determined by what genre the text is and what it seeks to do. A psalm often seeks to invite readers or listeners into a journey of lament that ends in praise. A proverb offers itself to listeners as a moral flashlight to shine on specific situations in daily life. An apocalyptic text seeks to impart a sense of urgency and compel readers to decision. A parable cracks open a window to get a glimpse of the different values operative in the kingdom of God and causes us to question our habitual attitudes and actions in light of it. An Old Testament narrative, or a story from one of the Gospels, invites us into the life story of an imperfect person in order to identify both with that person's weaknesses and the power of God at work through them. A good question is this: What kind of ending will allow this text to have the impact on listeners that it seeks to have?

The advice I've given on endings is pertinent to the following forms of sermons: text shaped, inductive, Lowry Loop, Four Pages, and Celebration. They all end with some presentation of the Good News. The preacher needs to ask herself: What is the most fitting way to end this sermon? Do I want to summarize its teachings, tell a story, complete a story, hold up an image, inspire listeners' emotions with eloquent, poetic language, suggest a specific line of action, invite listeners into a scene either biblical or contemporary, tie up loose ends, or challenge hearers with a question? Whatever choice I make, I need to be sure I have rehearsed my ending carefully, that I have chosen my words carefully, and that I haven't chosen too many words.

A fitting ending to this chapter on endings is to visit the four Gospels. Matthew, whose purpose is to form disciples that follow the teachings of Jesus, offers a "So now what?" ending to his Gospel in which Jesus, having assured the disciples of his power and continued presence with them, tells them what to do (Matt. 28:16–20). Mark, whose purpose is to form disciples willing to make tough choices and to suffer as Jesus suffered, presents us with an open-ended ending "So they went out and fled from the tomb, for terror and amazement had seized them; and they said nothing to anyone, for they were afraid." Luke, whose purpose is to form disciples who have compassion for the poor and the outcast, employs the celebration ending, in which we are invited to experience the joy that comes from service (Luke 24:50–53). John, whose purpose is to form disciples who believe in Jesus, features a story near the end of his Gospel that is intended to inspire belief: the story of the risen

Jesus appearing to his disciples and sharing a breakfast of fish and bread with them (John 21:9–14).

If endings tailored to one's purpose that are short though not necessarily sweet are good enough for the four evangelists, I believe they are good enough for us.

Questions for Reflection

1. Have I practiced my ending repeatedly so that I can deliver it with emotion, precision, and confidence?
2. Does my ending go on too long?
3. Do I send signals about ending the sermon that turn out to be false?
4. Is my ending repetitive? Do I tell people things I've already equipped them to figure out for themselves?
5. Have I begun a new sermon as I should be ending it?
6. Have I revisited the problem when I should be fleshing out the implications of the Good News?
7. Have I followed a dramatic story with dull and unnecessary explanation?
8. Have I given my sermon too tidy and shallow an ending, one that is not true to people's life experiences or that offers false promises that are not true to the biblical witness?
9. Have I told people what is wrong with them and badgered them to improve themselves without pointing them toward the Grace of God by which alone repentance and sanctification are possible?
10. Have I ended with the image or story with which I began?
11. Have I offered moral guidance in the context of Grace?
12. Have I told a story that embodies the focus of my sermon and encourages listeners to contextualize the sermon in scenes from their own lives?
13. Have I summarized the key teachings of the sermon in brief, vivid phrases?
14. Does the logic and emotional tone of the ending fit the theme and tone of the sermon?
15. Does the form I've chosen for my ending match the purpose of my sermon?

Reference List

Aden, LeRoy H., and Robert G. Hughes. 2002. *Preaching God's Compassion*. Minneapolis: Fortress Press.

Allen, O. Wesley, Jr. 2005. *The Homiletic of All Believers: A Conversation Approach*. Louisville, KY: Westminster John Knox Press.

Allen, Ronald J. 2008. "Theology Undergirding Narrative Preaching." In *What's the Shape of Narrative Preaching*, edited by Mike Graves and David J. Schlafer. St. Louis: Chalice Press.

———. 2004. *Hearing the Sermon: Relationship, Content, and Feeling*. St. Louis: Chalice Press.

———. 2002. *Preaching Is Believing: The Sermon as Theological Reflection*. Louisville, KY: Westminster John Knox Press.

———. 1998. *Interpreting the Gospel: An Introduction to Preaching*. St. Louis: Chalice Press.

Bartlett, David. 1999. *Between the Bible and the Church: New Methods for Biblical Preaching*. Nashville: Abingdon Press.

Becker, Norbert V. 1973. *Pitfalls in Preaching: Fifteen Common Weaknesses with Suggestions for More Dynamic and Relevant Preaching*. Christian Literature Society of the Philippines.

Berger, Daniel R. 2007. *Speaking the Truth in Love: Christian Public Rhetoric*. Eugene, OR: Wipf & Stock Publishers.

Bradley, Lorna. 2010. "Fully Puzzling" (sermon on Luke 9:28–36, preached as part of a doctor of ministry class at Perkins School of Theology, January 2010).

Brooks, Phillips. 1969. *Lectures on Preaching*. Grand Rapids: Baker Book House.

Brueggemann, Walter. 2003. *The Bible Makes Sense*. Rev. ed. Cincinnati: St. Anthony Messenger Press.

Burke, Kenneth. 1973. *The Philosophy of Literary Form: Studies in Symbolic Action*. 3rd ed., rev. Berkeley: University of California Press.

———. 1969. *A Rhetoric of Motives*. Berkeley, CA: University of California Press.

Buttrick, David. 1987. *Homiletic: Moves and Structures*. Minneapolis: Augsburg Fortress Press.

Cooper, Burton Z and John S. McClure. 2003. *Claiming Theology in the Pulpit*. Louisville, KY: Westminster John Knox Press.

Craddock, Fred. 2001. *As One Without Authority*. St. Louis: Christian Board of Publication.

————. 1985. *Preaching*. Nashville: Abingdon Press.

————. 1978. *Overhearing the Gospel*. Nashville: Abingdon Press.

Davis, Ellen F., and Richard B. Hayes. 2003. *The Art of Reading Scripture*. Grand Rapids: Wm. B. Eerdmans Publishing Co.

Davis, H. Grady. 1958. *Design for Preaching*. Minneapolis: Augsburg Fortress Press.

Day, David. 2006. *Preaching with All You've Got: Embodying the Word*. Peabody, MA: Hendrickson Publishers.

Denison, Charles. 2006. *The Artist's Way of Preaching*. Louisville, KY: Westminster John Knox Press.

Eslinger, Richard. 1996. *Pitfalls in Preaching*. Grand Rapids: Wm. B. Eerdmans Publishing Co.

Fleer, David, and Dave Bland, eds. 2001. *Preaching Autobiography: Connecting the World of the Preacher and the World of the Text*. Abilene, TX: Abilene Christian University Press.

Florence, Anna Carter. 2007. *Preaching as Testimony*. Louisville, KY: Westminster John Knox Press.

Gregory the Great. 1894. "Catalogue of Hearers," *The Book of Pastoral Rule*, Part III, 1-3, 8, trans. James Barmby, vol. 12 of *A Select Library of Nicene and Post-Nicene Fathers of the Christian Church*. New York: The Christian Literature Co.

Hodgson, Peter C., and Robert H. King, eds. 1982. *Christian Theology: An Introduction to Its Traditions and Tasks*. Philadelphia: Fortress Press.

Hogan, Lucy Lind, and Robert Reid. 1999. *Connecting with the Congregation: Rhetoric and the Art of Preaching*. Nashville: Abingdon Press.

Holbert, John. 1999. *Preaching Job*. St. Louis: Chalice Press.

Kastner, Patricia Wilson. 1989. *Imagery for Preaching*. Minneapolis: Fortress Press.

Langhofer, Steve. 2008. "Cleaning Up Your Mess" (sermon preached during Lent 2008 at Asbury United Methodist Church, Overland Park, Kansas).

Long, Thomas G. 2005. *The Witness of Preaching*. 2nd ed. Louisville, KY: Westminster John Knox Press.

————. 1989. *Preaching and the Literary Forms of the Bible*. Louisville, KY: Westminster John Knox Press.

Loscalzo, Craig. 1992. *Preaching Sermons That Connect: Effective Communication through Identification*. Downers Grove, IL: InterVarsity Press.

Lowry, Eugene.1980. *The Homiletical Plot*. Atlanta: John Knox Press.

Maddox, Randy L. 1994. *Responsible Grace: John Wesley's Practical Theology*. Nashville: Kingswood Books.

McClure, John S., ed. 1998. *Best Advice for Preaching*. Minneapolis: Fortress Press.

————. 1995. *The Roundtable Pulpit: Where Leadership and Preaching Meet*. Nashville: Abingdon Press.

McKenzie, Alyce M. 2010. *Novel Preaching: Tips from Top Writers on Crafting Creative Sermons*. Louisville, KY: Westminster John Knox Press.

————. 2008. "Finders Weepers, Losers Keepers" (sermon preached July 20, 2008, at Trietsch Memorial United Methodist Church, Flower Mound, Texas).

————. 2007a. "Nobody Else" (sermon preached January 21, 2007, at First United Methodist Church, Allen, Texas).

————. 2007b. *The Parables for Today*. Louisville, KY: Westminster John Knox Press.

————. 2004. *Preaching Biblical Wisdom in a Self-Help Society*. Nashville: Abingdon Press.

Mellette, Jonathan. 2010. "The Extraordinary" (sermon preached January 22, 2010, based on John 2:1–11).

Mitchell, Henry H. 1990. *Black Preaching: The Recovery of a Powerful Art*. Nashville: Abingdon Press.

Mulligan, Mary Alice, Diane Turner-Sharazz, Dawn Ottoni Wilhelm, and Ronald J. Allen, eds. 2005. *Believing in Preaching: What Listeners Hear in Sermons*. St. Louis: Chalice Press.

Mulligan Mary Alice, and Ronald J. Allen. 2005. *Make the Word Come Alive: Lessons from Laity*. St. Louis: Chalice Press.

Nieman, James R., and Thomas G. Rogers. 2001. *Preaching to Every Pew: Cross-Cultural Strategies*. Minneapolis: Fortress Press.

Pagitt, Doug. 2005. *Preaching Re-Imagined: The Role of the Sermon in Communities of Faith*. Grand Rapids: Zondervan.

Powell, Mark Allen. 2007. *What Do They Hear? Bridging the Gap between Pulpit and Pew*. Nashville: Abingdon Press.

Ramsey, G. Lee, Jr. 2000. *Care-Full Preaching*. St. Louis: Chalice Press.

Schlafer, David J. 1992. *Surviving the Sermon: A Guide to Preaching for Those Who Have to Listen*. Boston: Cowley Publications.

Shepherd, J. Barrie. 2006. *Whatever Happened to Delight? Preaching the Gospel in Poetry and Parables*. Louisville, KY: Westminster John Knox Press.

Sullivan, John. 2009. "Rhetoric and Preaching" (unpublished paper presented September 3, 2009, at a colloquy at Liverpool Hope University, Liverpool, England, on "Preaching John Wesley's Holy Living to Postmodern People").

Switzer, David. 1979. *Pastor, Preacher, Person*. Nashville: Abingdon Press.

Taylor, Gardner C. 1994. "His Own Clothes." In *A Chorus of Witnesses: Model Sermons for Today's Preacher*, edited by Thomas G. Long and Cornelius Plantinga Jr. Grand Rapids: Wm. B. Eerdmans Publishing Co.

Thomas, Frank. A. 1997. *They Like to Never Quit Praisin' God: The Role of Celebration in Preaching*. Cleveland: Pilgrim Press.

Thulin, Richard L. 1989. *The "I" of the Sermon*. Minneapolis: Augsburg Publishing House.

Tisdale, Nora Tubbs. 1998. "God's No and Ours." In *Patterns of Preaching: A Sermon Sampler*, edited by Ronald J. Allen. St. Louis: Chalice Press.

———. 1997. *Preaching as Local Theology and Folk Art*. Louisville, KY: Westminster John Knox Press.

Troeger, Thomas. 1982. *Creating Fresh Images for Preaching*. Valley Forge, PA: Judson Press.

Turner, Mary Donovan. 2003. *Old Testament Words: Reflections for Preaching*. St. Louis: Chalice Press.

Untener, Ken. 1999. *Preaching Better: Practical Advice for Homilists*. New York: Paulist Press.

Weatherhead, Leslie. 1990. *The Will of God*. New ed. New York: Hyperion Books.

Wesley, John. 1830. "Letter on Preaching Christ" (December 20, 1751). In *The Works of the Reverend John Wesley, A.M.*, Vol. 11. 3rd ed. London: John Mason.

Willimon, William H. 1994. "What Time Is It?" In *A Chorus of Witnesses: Model Sermons for Today's Preacher*. Grand Rapids: Wm. B. Eerdmans Publishing Co.

———. 1981. *Integrative Preaching*. Nashville: Abingdon Press.

Willobee, Sondra. 2009. *The Write Stuff: Crafting Sermons That Capture and Convince*. Louisville, KY: Westminster John Knox Press.

Wilson, Paul Scott. 2008. *Setting Words on Fire: Putting God at the Center of the Sermon.* Nashville: Abingdon Press.

————. 2007. *The Practice of Preaching.* Rev. ed. Nashville: Abingdon Press.

————. 2004. *Broken Words: Reflections on the Craft of Preaching.* Nashville: Abingdon Press.

————. 1999. *The Four Pages of the Sermon: A Guide to Biblical Preaching.* Nashville: Abingdon Press.

Wood, Charles M. 2008. *The Question of Providence.* Louisville, KY: Westminster John Knox Press.

251

H723ω

CPSIA information can be obtained at www.ICGtesting.com
Printed in the USA
LVOW10s1359020214

371966LV00015B/787/P